How to Build the MASTER SCHEDULE in 10 EASY STEPS

This book is dedicated to those who have enriched my life and made it so meaningful: the members of my family. It is a small sign of appreciation to let them know how very much they mean to me.

To Sharyn—my wife, soul mate, and best friend; to our "life's work" together—sons Todd, Eric, and Lonnie, as well as Todd's wife Alyssa and their daughter Rebecca Hayley; and to my parents, Bea and Lou—always there for me and now their memory will forever remain with our family.

To my wife, to my children, to my parents: Thank you; this honor belongs to you.

How to Build the MASTER SCHEDULE in 10 EASY STEPS

A Guide
for
Secondary
School
Administrators

STEVEN S. KUSSIN

CORWIN PRESS
A SAGE Publications Company
Thousand Oaks, CA 91320

For information:

Corwin Press
A Sage Publications Company
2455 Teller Road
Thousand Oaks, California 91320
www.corwinpress.com

Sage Publications Ltd.
1 Oliver's Yard
55 City Road
London EC1Y 1SP
United Kingdom

Sage Publications India Pvt. Ltd.
B 1/I 1 Mohan Cooperative Industrial Area
Mathura Road, New Delhi 110 044
India

Sage Publications Asia-Pacific Pte. Ltd.
33 Pekin Street #02-01
Far East Square
Singapore 048763

Printed in the United States of America

Library of Congress Cataloging-in-Publication Data

Kussin, Steven.
How to build the master schedule in 10 easy steps: A guide for secondary school administrators/Steven S. Kussin.
   p. cm.
ISBN 978-1-4129-5590-4 (cloth)
ISBN 978-1-4129-5591-1 (pbk.)
   1. Schedules, School—United States—Administration—Handbooks, manuals, etc.
2. High schools—United States—Administration—Handbooks, manuals, etc. I. Title.

LB3032.K87 2008
373.12'42—dc22

2007007911

This book is printed on acid-free paper.

07 08 09 10 11 12 10 9 8 7 6 5 4 3 2 1

Acquisitions Editor:	Elizabeth Brenkus
Editorial Assistants:	Desirée Enayati and Ena Rosen
Production Editor:	Jenn Reese
Copy Editor:	Kristin Bergstad
Typesetter:	C&M Digitals (P) Ltd.
Cover Designer:	Michael Dubowe
Graphic Designer:	Lisa Riley

Contents

Acknowledgments

After building schedules and running workshops for more than thirty years, I wanted to commit to paper the ideas I have been sharing with hundreds of administrators and supervisors—with the hope that future generations of educational leaders will benefit from this experience.

There are some people who deserve my heartfelt thanks for making this book possible.

To my wife Sharyn, who is my partner and adviser in anything and everything I do; to our three sons Todd, Eric, and Lonnie, who not only have been my inspiration, but have also made me so proud by being everything a father could ask for; to our granddaughter Rebecca Hayley, who always makes me smile, born to Todd and his wife Alyssa; and finally, to my parents, Bea and Lou Kussin, who spared nothing to provide me the best possible education and every opportunity imaginable.

My first editor, Lizzie Brenkus, was a sheer delight to work with, always extremely helpful, enthusiastic, and encouraging. Desirée Enayati, editorial assistant, never tired of answering my production questions and responding to my e-mails. Kristin Bergstad, copy editor, meticulously read every word (and number!) in the text, constantly providing valuable feedback and excellent suggestions. Jenn Reese, production editor, took my book the last mile, creatively and diligently delivering it to the finish line. What a highly professional team, every step of the way.

I would also like to acknowledge my close friend and colleague, John Pancia, whom we lost in October 2006. John was a wordsmith and proofreader par excellence, who taught me the tricks of the trade. If I was nicknamed the "grammar policeman," then he was the "lieutenant."

Corwin Press gratefully acknowledges the contributions of the following individuals:

Robert Blake, Principal
Mainland Regional High School, Linwood, NJ

Judy Brunner, Educational Consultant
Edu-Safe LLC, Springfield, MO

Lexy Conte, Principal
Amargosa Creek Middle School, Lancaster, CA

Robert Frick, Superintendent
Lampeter-Strasburg School District, Lampeter, PA

G. Steven Griggs, Director of Student Services & Operations
Francis Howell School District, St. Charles, MO

Robert Hess, Student Achievement Leader
Springfield Schools, Springfield, OR

Ann Ogletree, Facilitator, Distance Learning Program
University of Cincinnati, Cincinnati, OH

David L. Sechler, Middle School Principal, retired
Dover, DE

Michelle L. Tichy, Professor
St. Norbert College, De Pere, WI

About the Author

Steven S. Kussin is Adjunct Professor in the School of Communications at Hofstra University and has taught at New York University and C.W. Post College as well. He received his Bachelor of Arts from Cornell University, his Master of Science from Brooklyn College, and his Doctor of Philosophy from New York University. He has been an educator for thirty-seven years, including twenty-one years as a high school principal. Kussin has been building master schedules for more than thirty years. In addition to running workshops on "How to Build the Master Schedule" throughout the greater New York metropolitan area, he serves as an education consultant to a number of school districts. Since 2006, he has been writing a weekly column on education titled the "Principal's Office." It appears in the Herald newspaper chain on Long Island.

Photo by
Stephan Kravitz.

Kussin resides in Merrick, Long Island, New York, with his wife of thirty-five years, Sharyn, who was a Spanish teacher in New York City. The couple has three sons: Todd, Eric, and Lonnie (all of whom also attended Cornell). Todd and his wife Alyssa are the parents of Rebecca Hayley. In his spare time, Kussin likes being "Grandpa," volunteering for several community causes, playing the piano, and writing. He is currently completing a novel that he plans to turn into a screenplay.

Author's Note

I have been running "How to Build the Master Schedule" workshops since 1976. Attendees and colleagues are forever asking, "Don't you ever get *bored* doing the same thing after more than thirty years?" On the contrary! I liken the experience to a tour guide taking his guests on a trip through his country. The enthusiasm never wanes. Then there's the "Eureka!" phenomenon: Many educators come to my classes with absolutely no knowledge of scheduling, but by the end of the day they have at least a rudimentary knowledge of the process. For a teacher to constantly hear his students say, "I got it!" is most rewarding. I hope that in the pages that follow, you will also "get it." I make every effort to reduce this complex process to a science— and maybe even an art. I have always maintained that you can learn a great deal about a school just by looking at its master schedule. Every effort should be made to make yours the best it can possibly be. To that end this book is directed.

Introduction

How to Use This Book

Perhaps no task is more challenging (or more intimidating) to a school administrator than that of building the master schedule. There have been few if any definitive texts written about this complex process—probably because it is so difficult to pin down. Find two school systems, and invariably you will find two different ways of doing business. What works in a large urban school setting doesn't necessarily do the job for its suburban counterpart. What holds for a middle-size rural school doesn't necessarily hold for a summer school or alternative program.

This book takes an altogether different approach. Rather than recommending a single scheduling strategy or addressing one specific population, it instead presents the "generic" brand. What follows are *ten steps to building the master schedule*, with a separate chapter devoted to each step. It must be underscored that these ten steps will be applicable to *any* situation: urban or suburban . . . city or rural . . . large or small . . . high school, junior high, or middle school . . . public, private, or parochial . . . conventional secondary or small learning community. These ten steps work for everyone, from the most traditional to experimental and alternative schools with block scheduling. Nobody is left out.

Nor will it matter whether the school reorganizes once a year (annual promotion) or twice a year (semiannual promotion). For example, with the exception of half-year electives, most courses in my suburban area run for a full year; just across the border in New York City, most high schools reschedule for both September and February. But the differences don't stop there. Some schools reorganize/reschedule three times (trimesters), four times (quadmesters), or even five times a year (quinmesters). No problem: *The basic ten scheduling steps remain the same.* In the latter cases, however, the same ten would have to be followed three, four, or even five times a year. Yes, some adaptations will have to be made for each particular school or district. Nevertheless, the basic ten stay the same.

Similarly, this book is meant to be read by those new to scheduling as well as by experienced veterans. Each of the ten steps is methodically explained and is illustrated with several concrete examples readily understandable to novices. Even practitioners who have mastered schedule building should be able to pick up some new tips, tricks, and techniques along the way. I know that I have learned some novel ways of doing things from my students in the course of thirty years of running workshops.

Navigating This Book: Organization

Each chapter opens with an *introduction* listing the objectives of that step and culminates with a *summary* and list of *tasks* to be completed. Generous use of *headings* is made for easier reading. *Charts* and *tables* with simulated data illustrate each point. *Exercises* are provided to test your knowledge of the new material. There is also a series of *helpful hints,* practical tips that have made my job easier and me more efficient—and hopefully will prove equally helpful for you. My Mom read "Helpful Household Hints from Heloise." Well, these are practical *scheduling* ideas from *me.* *Sample forms* are provided that can be readily adapted for your individual needs. Finally, *footnotes* are included to provide additional examples and personal anecdotes.

Caveats

As was noted, this book was designed for secondary school administrators from coast to coast. There are some significant differences among schools systems, but none that affect the ten steps themselves. To make the examples and illustrations universally applicable, I used the most common parameters. If yours are different, no problem; adjust accordingly. For example:

1. In discussing the twelve-month scheduling cycle, I use the September-to-June model. In some parts of the country, however, districts operate on an August-to-May calendar. Just realign the dates to meet your needs. Move up the suggested deadlines to make them work for your own situation.

2. I use eight- or nine-period days for many examples. If your schools uses something different (four double periods for block scheduling or an extended day with ten or more periods), adjust accordingly.

3. Deadlines for the school budget can have a bearing on the staffing issues. Again, a nonissue. Adjust the suggested deadlines to make them fit your needs. The "what" (i.e., the content of the discussions) is more important than the "when."

4. From coast to coast (and even within the same regions), school administrators don't speak the same language: the same jobs, the same procedures—but different labels. For example: department heads, chairpersons, lead teachers . . . academic, college prep, regular classes . . . general, skills level, third track . . . leveling, balancing, equalizing classes . . . years, units, credits . . . are just a few of the many different labels for the exact same concepts. Use what works for you. Shakespeare asked, "What's in a name?" So do I: nothing.

Theory Versus Practice

As promised from the start, this book is heavily skewed toward *practice,* not *theory.* Heavily, but not totally. A few theoretical points need to be made. Several theories in educational leadership maintain that the administrator must possess three skills in order to be successful: conceptual . . . technical . . . and interpersonal. Nothing proves this to be true more than building the master schedule.

I always ask my students the rhetorical question: "What does a three-legged stool need to stand?" The answer is obvious: the strength of *all three legs.* Two, no matter how strong, are not enough without the third; without the third leg, the stool will topple. This is clearly illustrated with the schedule-building model. The schedule-builder must *conceptualize* the way the organization (in this case, the district and school) is run: its power bases, hierarchy, roles, and relationships. There must be a global view of "how things run around here" and "what makes this place tick." Second, the scheduler must master the *technical* skills requisite for building the schedule. Before putting pencil to paper, he[1] must be familiar with preregistration figures, enrollment projections, tallies, conflict matrices, simulation figures—just to name a few. In short, he must know the tools of the trade *and* how to use them. Third and finally, there has to be some understanding of people. Here, *interpersonal* skills and human relations come into play. Manipulating the above-mentioned conceptual and technical variables will entail a huge number of interactions with superiors, colleagues, and subordinates. How effectively those connections are made will affect the quality of the finished product.

To repeat: Two without the third just won't work. I have known colleagues who grasp the concepts (the global picture) and master the technical tasks (the detail work); but it is their interpersonal relations (or lack thereof) that bring them down. Similarly, I have come across schedulers who are masters of human relations—but sloppy with their technical work; they, too, encounter difficulties that could have been avoided. Finally, there are administrators who know the technical stuff, deal well with people—but fail to see the larger picture, the conceptual. Yes, that includes the political. One more time: A three-legged stool needs three sturdy legs on which to stand.

We just discussed what the master schedule *is*. Just as important, we also need to see what the schedule-building process *isn't*. There was a time when it was viewed as a job delegated to the low person on the totem pole who had to pay administrative dues. At my scheduling seminars, I always begin by asking the participants to explain why they've come. Many sheepishly confess that they were sent, having being assigned the task/chore/burden of building the schedule next year—almost as if it were a punishment. Whoever gets stuck with the job visualizes being exiled to a remote corner of the school building at the end of the school year, stocked with pencils, paper, and coffee rations, and sternly warned not to resurface until a finished master schedule is in hand. The entire process is performed over a relatively short period of time in complete isolation. Nothing could be farther from the truth.

The schedule-building process is to be viewed as a ten-step, twelve-month interactive process of interfacing with every other office of the school. As we shall see in the sections to follow, the process starts in the fall of one school year . . . and ends in the fall of the next school year—just in time to start all over again. It involves two-way communication with just about every branch of the school's organization: central office personnel, building administrators, department heads, guidance counselors, attendance supervisors, grade reporting teams, and data processing units. Don't worry if the people in your school have different job titles; what's important is that the jobs get done.

Depending on the size of the school system, one person may wear two or more hats. It doesn't matter. What *is* important is that the scheduler exchanges complete and accurate information with the right people at the appropriate times. As we shall see, the domino effect looms over the scheduling process; even a simple mistake at the beginning can have far-reaching (and potentially disastrous) effects down the line.

---

[1] I will avoid the politically correct-but cumbersome-he/she references. Rather, I will alternate between "he" and "she" when using pronouns referring to our cast of characters.

√ Helpful Hint 1

Here comes the first of those practical tips I said I'd be passing along.

More and more schools are forming a scheduling committee to deal with some of the policy issues that will come up. You will come across many of these in the pages that follow.

- In some schools, these issues are decided by the principal and his colleagues.
- In others, they are up for discussion among the members of the principal's cabinet, including the department heads.
- In still others, there is a shared decision-making team or site-based management committee that will be delegated these responsibilities.
- And as just stated, some schools create scheduling committees empowered to make many of the choices that will come up. Such committees can include any constituencies deemed appropriate: administration, supervision, rank-and-file teachers, teachers' association, clerical/data processing, parents, students. While not all of these have to be part of the committee, there are advantages to making it inclusive, as we shall see.

Definitions

There are certain variables that *must* be defined before we begin, because they may vary even from school to school within the same district.

Elective

The first term is *elective*. It can have *three* very different meanings. All three definitions reflect the course requirements in a particular school. The *first* definition of elective is "in lieu of." For example, all twelfth graders are probably required to take some form of Senior English. In some schools, however, they may *elect* to take Creative Writing or Advanced Placement (AP) English *in lieu of* the required course. The *second* definition of elective is the course taken "in addition to" the required course. In another school, Creative Writing may not be taken *in lieu of* Senior English—but can be taken *in addition to it* for elective credit. Another example: Students may be required to complete three years (*or* credits *or* units) of mathematics; however, they may opt to continue with elective courses in that department, such as Computer Programming or Statistics. The *third* definition of elective covers courses taken for elective credit only. In many high schools, Business Education per se doesn't appear at all in the graduation requirements, yet students may *elect* to take such courses as Keyboarding or Accounting for *elective* credit. Often, those departments live or die based on student demand for their courses. More on that below. Electives will be a key variable in the process. All three definitions will be used in this text; it should be clear as to which definition is meant.

A bit more about electives: Some high schools offer mostly required/core courses and only a smattering of electives. Social Studies provides a good example. With a four-year requirement in many states, the department may offer few, if any, electives. For an elective to survive, there must be enough students willing to double up and take two courses in that department. This is a perfect example of definition 2: the in-addition-to elective. When that's the case, then courses such as Sociology and Ethnic Studies might flourish. If students are not willing to spend their elective choices on those courses, the courses won't survive. Generally, English, Math, and Science also fall into this category; they consist largely of required courses with the number of in-addition-to electives varying from school to school.

Foreign Language (aka Second Language and World Language) varies the most. Depending on the state (or even the school system within the same state), it may exist by offering required courses—or courses that are purely elective. *Is completing one or more courses/credits/units/years in Language part of the diploma requirements?* The answer will determine how this department operates. Fine Arts, Music, Technology, Business Education, and Home Economics (a department also operating under several aliases) tend to be largely elective in nature and survive based on student demand. Some states do not require any courses whatsoever in these departments.

Now, a word or two about that student demand. At this point we need to introduce the "elective pie." Its size remains constant (unless the school adds an additional period of instruction). Suppose, for example, the school runs an eight-period day with students required to have a lunch period. That means a student takes a maximum of seven classes. Put another way, students have just so much room for adding electives beyond the requirements. The size of each elective department is determined by competition to draw students and increase (or at least maintain) its share of the elective pie. To be blunt, it becomes a case of survival of the fittest. Departments with the most appealing electives will flourish, while those with less attractive offerings will wither. This is not always a popular thing to say, but it is true. I was once called in and asked why the Home Economics Department in a high school was steadily losing students, sections, and staff. It didn't take long to figure out why. The outdated program took on the look of Betty Crocker's kitchen, circa 1950. Nothing had been done to update the program beyond Cooking and Baking. Furthermore, there were few if any boys. The department head was referred to a neighboring school where the Family and Consumer Science Department (new name) featured modern courses in Single Survival, International Foods, and Adolescent Psychology.

One more example: Another district in which students had five foreign languages from which to pick asked why one of them was dying. All they had to do was take a look at the program itself to see why it didn't appeal to students, at least as it compared to the other four competing programs. Sadly, the teacher had lost interest and was running the program into the ground; he could not compete with the enthusiasm his colleagues displayed toward their subject matter. Some object to my using the term *competing*. Like it or not, it's a fact of life. Put yourself in the shoes of a student reaching the senior year; with one (or at the most two) spaces in the schedule open for electives, how is she going to choose? It *is* survival of the fittest.

School Organization

We also have to define the way secondary schools are organized. Readers of this book run the gamut from teachers in charge of small alternative schools to principals of large high schools with several thousand students. Remember what I said at the top about the generic brand. Secondary schools are subdivided into departments. Here is a common model: English, Social Studies, Math, Science, Foreign Language, Fine Arts, Music, Technology, Home Economics (Family Consumer Science), Health and Physical Education, Special Education, Vocational Education. There is no one right way to organize a school; the examples used in the pages to follow are for illustrative purposes only; they don't profess what is correct. Mix and match 'em whichever way works best for your district. The good news is that the ten scheduling steps fit them all.

The point being made is that schools organize their departments in a variety of ways:

- There may be a separate Reading Department. Or, Reading and English may be combined in a single department called Language Arts.
- Computer Science may be a separate department—or part of the Math or Business Education Departments.
- As already noted, Foreign Language may be called Second Language, Languages Other Than English, or World Languages.
- English as a Second Language and/or Bilingual Education may be stand-alone departments or subsumed under the Foreign Language Department.
- Technology may be merged with Home Economics (or one of its aliases).
- Vocational, Occupational, and Career Education may be separate departments—or combined with Technology.
- Even Fine Arts and Industrial Arts may be combined into a single department.
- Ditto for Fine Arts and Music.
- Health and Physical Education may be separate or combined departments and may also include Drivers Education.
- Business Education may be an umbrella for Accounting, Secretarial Studies, and Career Education. Or, each of these may be a separate department.

Time

The third and final set of definitions has to do with the variable *time*. The fact that schools may reorganize anywhere from one to five times a year has already been mentioned. Most schools employ annual or semiannual promotion; tri-, quad-, and quinmesters are far less common. This variable does not matter to us. The only thing we need to know is that the *same ten steps* will be followed one, two, three, four, or five times during the school year. Just keep in mind the effect these differences can have on course titles and the resulting confusion that can ensue if not thought out carefully. Spanish "2" in a school on annual promotion means second-year Spanish; but that same course title in a school on semiannual promotion means the second semester of first-year Spanish.

√ Helpful Hint 2

One more bit of advice before we get started: Invest in a spiral-bound or a "marble" composition notebook. Use it as a diary. Chronicle, on a daily basis, every scheduling function you perform. At the beginning of the year, there may be days at a time when there are no entries; however, when the scheduling process reaches its peak during the second semester, there will be several entries for some days. In addition, annotate the log. Indicate what went right . . . what went wrong . . . and what you could have done better. Learn from your mistakes so you don't make them again. Indicate what you would have done differently if you had a second chance—because you will have another chance—the following year.

The first time around, it may be a bit difficult to record every scheduling activity. Do it; don't skip a day. Maintaining this log is well worth the effort. If you keep this notebook up to date, after the first year and one complete scheduling cycle, it will make the second time around so much easier. By the third year, you will be a pro. Not only will this timeline remind you what comes next, but your comments will help you to do things more effectively and more efficiently.

So much for the preliminaries. *The ten steps about to be presented work in all settings.* We're done with the theory, we've covered all the definitions, we speak a common language. Fasten your seat belt! We're ready to embark on the twelve-month, ten-step scheduling odyssey.

Step 1

Plan It

The Curriculum Development Phase

Many years ago when I incorporated excerpts of this book into my scheduling workshop, a mythical high school named for a prominent early American was used for the simulations and exercises. Soon after, a complaint was lodged by the "real" school with the same name. No offense was meant. However, to avoid any potential misunderstandings, we will use "USA High School" for the examples to follow—with the hope that no one will take exception to *that* name.

Menu Planning

Let's get started. It's February and you have just received the good news that you have been named the first principal of USA High School, projected to open the following fall. You have a clean slate, a fresh start. All that you know is that come September, you must be ready to open a new building for 1,200 students. Your mission is to build its master schedule. Where do you begin? What is the first step?

I always pose this question to would-be schedulers. Generally, they respond by getting busy with the timetable itself: periods, sections, and teachers. Premature. This will all come later. It is much too early to discuss those variables. As we shall see, the timetable per se is only the tip of the iceberg; there is much more information beneath the surface that needs to be worked out. Some critical decisions must be made first.

Suppose you were going to open a brand new restaurant. What's the first thing you'd need to know? You'd have to determine what type it would be. Italian pizzeria? French cuisine? Kosher deli? What's the menu? Before ordering, planning, hiring, advertising, cooking, and serving, you have to know *what* it is you are going to offer.

The same holds true for scheduling. *The first step in building the master schedule is selecting the menu. What is your program of study? What courses are you going to offer? Step 1, then, is the "Plan It" or Curriculum Development Phase.* For a brand new school, you must start from scratch, and for established schools the process is basically the same. Once a year, take stock of what exists: Evaluate the old and propose the new. It's time to add, delete, and modify existing courses.

Deciding on the "what" is only the beginning. There is a series of concomitant questions to be answered. Remember our restaurant analogy? You might have decided on an Italian restaurant. But is it fast food? Buffet? Or, fine dining? These are a few of the key questions you need to answer before proceeding.

- What is the curriculum to be studied for each course in every department?
- How are these classes to be organized?
- How will the students be grouped?
- At what level(s) will they learn?
- At what rate(s) will the teachers be teaching?

Let's illustrate with two concrete examples. Suppose that 300 ninth graders are coming to USA High School when it opens. It is a safe assumption that all of them will be taking some version of English 9/Freshman English. But that's the *only* thing you know so far. What are some of the options from which you can choose?

Before I present some of the possibilities, jot down a few of your own. Think outside of the box. Anything is possible. We'll use "30" as the class size. For some school systems, thirty may seem on the high side, for others it might be low. It's just a number. *It doesn't matter what your district uses!* The number thirty will work well for our examples. Back home, substitute what works in your district.[1]

1. Heterogeneous Classes. You can take the 300 students and divide them into ten classes of thirty students each. The sections will be heterogeneous in makeup and randomly formed. On paper, they are all the same.

2. Homogeneous Classes. You can go to the other extreme and ability group the 300 students based on reading scores and writing assessments. In this model, you can identify the top thirty scorers and put them in class "9–1," the honors group or whatever else you want to name it. At the other end of the achievement spectrum, you can count out the ninth graders most deficient in reading and writing skills and place them in class "9–10" or however you designate it. You might consider making this skills-deficient group somewhat smaller in size—but that type of decision can come later. For now, we'll make all of the ten classes thirty in size.

3. Tracking. It's become a dirty word in education, but *tracking* is another option. You can identify students as "honors," "academic/college prep," "general/skills," "remedial," "Special Ed," "ESL/limited English proficiency," or any other designation in your population. Depending on the composition of the student body, you can have a proportionate number of sections in each track. For example, one community might have a preponderance of "honors" and "college prep" sections while a neighboring district might require more "general" and "ESL/LEP" classes. In a college

---

[1] When I ran this workshop on the regional level, attendees included representatives from two neighboring districts, one part of a large city school district, the other an affluent independent suburban district just the other side of the city line. I used this class size of "30" for my examples. The urban school participants commented that their class sizes would never be so low; on the other hand, their suburban counterparts commented that their class sizes would never be so high. To repeat: It doesn't matter. The number "30" is a good compromise for illustrative purposes.

town, as many as half of the classes may be honors and AP (Advanced Placement); in a farming village down the road, there might be no honors classes at all. No problem; they are just different.

4. *Partial Elective Program.* So far we have been talking about bread 'n' butter courses. You might opt for a partial elective program. Designate several of the ten sections as special classes such as Journalism, Creative Writing, and Drama. The remaining seven sections would fall into one of the above-mentioned options.

5. *Total Elective Program.* You can decide to go with an all-elective program—even for ninth graders. One school of thought maintains that the primary objective of the English program is to get students to enjoy reading and writing, and that content is secondary. To that end, the ninth grade program would feature a series of half-year reading and writing electives. Students would select one of each. For example: Sports in Literature, Mythology, and Classics on the reading side; Creative Writing, Narrative Writing, and Grammar 101 on the writing side.

6. *Interdisciplinary.* One curriculum initiative now in vogue is to team English and Social Studies, given their interrelationship. Why teach the French Revolution in Social Studies . . . and *Tale of Two Cities* in English . . . separately?[2] The two should be taught in tandem. Social Studies is the tail that wags the dog, with the books in English having to follow the more prescribed curriculum of history and geography.

7. *Mix and Match.* Piece together a patchwork quilt using parts of any or all of these six or design *another* program deemed best for *your* set of circumstances.

I hope that you're beginning to get the idea of what the Plan It step is all about. We'll do a second exercise. Take the same thirty ninth graders, again assuming that you'll have ten sections of thirty students each, and design a *Mathematics* program for them. Once again, take a few moments to tackle this assignment by yourself before looking at the "answers" (i.e., list of options enumerated below).

Before we begin this exercise, we have to clear up one of those pesky language problems. Given: Most ninth grade math programs across our fifty states focus on elementary algebra, although the delivery tends to vary considerably. It doesn't matter which pattern *your* district follows. For simplicity's sake, we'll call the course "Algebra."

But even then it's not that simple. It's doubtful that you are going to be able to offer all of your ninth graders that same course. Remember, above we mentioned "grouping" and "rate." What, then, are some of the options to consider?

1. *Standard Two-Semester Algebra.* Odds are, most will be candidates for the conventional two-semester/yearlong Algebra course. Most, but not all. Schools with special populations may opt for some of the other options listed below.

2. *Three-Semester Algebra.* There may be some marginal students who would like to tackle this challenging course, but approach it with trepidation. Consider offering it at a slower pace, over a year and a half. Hence: Algebra—three semesters. Note that I said, "There *may* be . . ." You haven't been given this information yet. But include this choice on your menu.

---

[2]A colleague realized that his school was offering American Literature in grade 10 and American History in grade 11; conversely, World Literature was offered in grade 11—while World History was given in grade 10. This made absolutely no sense. It took considerable doing to flip flop American and World Lit and one year during which World Lit was taught in both grades, but the more logical pairing was successfully phased in after two years.

3. *Algebra—Double Period.* Obviously, the three-semester version is more expensive to offer (in terms of teacher time) than the two-semester. A double-period version is the most expensive. (We'll talk about budget and teacher time in Step 4.) For now, suffice it to say that two of a teacher's five[3] teaching periods will be devoted to this one section. And if there are two (or more) sections of the double-period version, be prepared to allocate even more of your staffing budget.

4. *Algebra—Continuation.* What about students who come to USA High School who started an Algebra course at the feeder school they attended previously? If that is the case, you will have to offer something like Algebra—Part 2.

5. *Algebra Honors/Accelerated.* There may be students who are recommended for an honors or accelerated version. How many of these sections will you need? At this point—you have no clue. Just put them on the menu. "Orders" have not been taken yet. You may end up with one or two . . . several . . . or none at all—depending on the makeup of the student population. That's not your concern, at least not *now*.

6. *Geometry.* Is there the possibility that some students have already completed Algebra in the eighth grade? You may have to offer ninth graders the course that follows Algebra, usually Geometry. To complicate matters, you may need an Honors version of this course as well. The menu is getting longer.

7. *Pre-Algebra/Algebra Prep.* There may be students for whom Algebra (even taught over three semesters or a double period) is too rigorous. They may require more foundations work. A Pre-Algebra or Algebra Prep course may be best for them.

8. *Nonacademic Math.* Then there may be some students for whom academic math is not appropriate at all. Alternatives such as Occupational Math, Business Math, or Consumer Math may be the best choices for them.

9. *Fundamentals.* You may have students so deficient in skills that a Fundamentals course, emphasizing remediation, is in order. This could be a regularly scheduled class or a math lab period built into their schedule. More permutations.

10. *Special Populations.* Don't forget about other populations such as Special Education (self-contained *and* inclusion), English as a Second Language, and bilingual. They must be scheduled for Math as well, and may require sections separate from those already listed.

While we listed ten alternatives, there are actually more, given all the permutations and subdivisions. But this is enough to reckon with for now. Wouldn't it be nice if all the 300 ninth graders simply took "Math 9"? Alas, that is not the case.

Criteria

Ten sections—ten options. One of each? Sorry, it's not that easy. Odds are, your school may not require all ten. We don't know yet what your customers will request.

---

[3] The vast majority of teachers teach five classes per day. However, there are exceptions. In some school systems, teachers teach six or only four. By now you've got the idea that for this scheduling text, it clearly doesn't matter. We're going to use "five" for illustrative purposes only.

Until orders are taken, they all remain on the menu. What are some of the criteria that will determine which of the options will ultimately be offered? These factors apply to *all* curriculum decisions across *all* departments in your school.

1. *Mandate.* Some courses are required; these are "givens." There is no question that they will be offered. For example, some states mandate a semester-long course in Health Education. On the other hand, there may be *no* mandate that students take a Business Education course. It is possible (although unlikely) that you end up with a master schedule without a single Business course. Certain departments survive depending on student interest. Much more on that subject below.

Other requirements vary from state to state. For example, in one state it might be "the law" that all students take four years of English . . . three of Social Studies. . . . two of Math . . . two of Science . . . a course in Career Education . . . and Physical Education. A neighboring state may not mandate Career Education—but instead requires one year of Foreign Language study. Yet another district demands *three* years of both Math and Science. Still another requires a course in writing. And another requires a course in its state history. And so it goes. Our purpose here is not to present a uniform set of mandates, but rather to know what to look for. In addition, you may have to establish programs for Special Education . . . Limited English Proficiency . . . Remediation—among others. To repeat: You have no choice as far as *mandated* courses are concerned.

2. *Student Ability.* You may put on the menu Advanced Placement courses in every subject that is offered. However, if you don't have students capable of handling this rigorous coursework, then these classes will not draw. On a more limited basis, in an established school, you may want to *add* an AP course. Let's use Chemistry for our example. If there are not enough students with the prerequisite coursework or grades for this most demanding subject, it's not going to fly.

3. *Student Interest.* Similarly, interest has to be there as well. Students have just so many elective choices to spend. You may have extremely capable students who are ideal candidates for AP Chemistry, but when it comes time for course selection, they'll have to make some tough decisions among competing courses. Perhaps there are other AP courses or electives they would rather take. Student ability is not enough. *Interest* is just as important. You may have enough students capable of taking AP Chemistry, but their interests may not lie there and the course may not fill.

4. *Resources.* When it comes to the curriculum, we're all like kids in the candy store. All those electives look tempting—and we'd like to add them to our shopping basket. However, from a practical standpoint, we have to talk about resources.
    o   If additional staff is needed for a new course, is it in the budget?
    o   What about equipment? Space? Books?
    o   Assuming those funds are available, is there a certified teacher who can teach the course? Go back to that AP Chemistry course. Finding *any* science teacher is tough enough; locating one capable of teaching AP is a greater challenge.[4]

---

[4] When I left for my first administrative job, I was teaching a specialized English elective called Mass Media. Money was not the issue. While there were monetary resources to continue the course with a replacement, the issue was finding the human resources, i.e. a qualified teacher with the training for this specialized elective.

5. *Community Values.* Suppose that there are students who are interested and capable of taking this new AP Chemistry course. Suppose that one of the science teachers has the training to teach the course. And suppose there are funds available to refurbish a science lab and purchase the necessary books and materials. There is one more variable that we must throw into the mix: community values. Is the community willing to expend its resources on this curriculum initiative? Let's say that thirteen students preregister for the course. As we shall see, that's a tricky number. In one district, it might be a no-brainer: A college-town community that puts a premium on education might not think twice about running the course regardless of the number of students signed up. On the other hand, a working-class town where education dollars don't come so easily might have a policy about the minimum number needed to run a new course. Two communities, the same set of variables, two very different outcomes. I must emphasize that there is no right or wrong answer. The community, which is footing the bill, becomes a major player in the decision-making process, and rightly so.

6. *Feasibility.* There is a sixth criterion that determines *what* will ultimately appear in the course of study. Let's say that the Business Education Department has been in decline in recent years, reduced to one teacher with five courses. The board of education, PTA, and administration all concur that with so many students interested in business, this department should be flourishing. For the next year, then, a slate of a dozen Business Education electives is offered. The board's collective heart was in the right place—but it was not *feasible* to go from "worst to first" so fast. By adding so many new courses, literally overnight, there was a splintering effect. No one single elective drew the double digits in preregistration enrollment needed to survive. As a result, most were canceled and the department was back to where it started. It would have been a better idea to introduce one or two new electives each year. After several years, the department would have been built back up gradually. As it was presented, it was too much, too fast.

√ Helpful Hint 3

We just spent considerable time cataloguing the key variables that must be considered when designing a school's course of study. Precisely *when* and *how* does this take place? Every high school needs to create a "curriculum review council" that will *collaboratively* make these decisions. The principal probably has a cabinet consisting of assistant principals and department heads. Or, you may choose to have the aforementioned "school scheduling committee" oversee this task. During October and early November, this group should change hats and become this curriculum review council. This annual exercise should be conducted every year without fail. The council should meet once a week until its work is accomplished. Each department representative should be prepared to make a presentation to the group as to any changes in the course of study in his or her department.

- What course(s) do you want to add? Drop? Modify?

Some departments may have no changes planned for next year, while others have extensive reports. This process continues until all have had a chance to present their proposals.

The Curriculum Review Council serves several purposes. *First*, it is a methodical, organized way to conduct an annual curriculum review. *Second*, it subscribes to the view that two heads are better than one. As a department rep reports, colleagues may see potential problems and pitfalls he didn't see. Take a proposed new elective in Computer Graphics: "Why not make it a semester-long elective rather than a full-year course?" Or, "Do we have enough computer stations to offer more than one section?" *Third*, there won't be any surprises down the road. For example, when the course catalogue is ultimately distributed, you don't want the Business Education teachers to find a course that they believe belongs to them in a different department. Nicely put, it prevents turf wars. For all of these reasons, the curriculum review (either by the cabinet or scheduling committee) must be a priority for October and early November.

I'm often asked about the role of teachers, parents, and students in the curriculum review process. This is a thorny issue, and one every district will have to grapple with on its own. Generally speaking, input from these constituencies can prove very valuable. For example, a September department meeting can be devoted to reviewing the course of study just for that department—with those recommendations delivered to the curriculum review council. The PTA and student council may wish to pass along information as well. It may be the parents who bemoan the demise of Business Education referred to above and provide the impetus to turn things around. Similarly, the student body might see some deficiencies, such as the need for more honors and AP courses. All of this information should be passed along to the council for its review. Note, I say "passed along." It is unwieldy to have too many people present at these meetings. Furthermore, once parents and students become full-fledged members, teachers understandably will want their own place at the table as well. Better to get these reports and have them submitted by one of the members. The only exception would be a special report by invitation. Otherwise, this is where the educational leadership should be delegated to make the best possible decisions.

Before we leave Step 1, one more word about the role of teachers. Most often, the ideas for new courses come from them. The problem is that they don't realize how far in advance the planning takes place; after all, if Macy's has to do its planning and purchasing several seasons ahead, why shouldn't schools do the same thing? It's frustrating when teachers excitedly approach the principal with great ideas for new courses. Alas, they are too late. To solve this problem, I offer . . .

√ Helpful Hint 4

Most principals write a regular newsletter or weekly bulletin for their faculty members. Mine was called *This Week*, and the staff found it in their mailboxes on Monday morning. This item appeared in the first issue of the new school year in September:

Believe It or Not: It's only the first day of school—but it's already time to start thinking about the schedule for the *next* school year. I want everyone to be aware of deadlines so we don't have to say "too late" when a great idea for a new course is submitted in December or January. These decisions will be made next month [October] when the Curriculum Review Council begins its annual job of going through the course of study. The first step is to speak to your department head. *Now!* The next step is to put something down on paper.

One more word about the curriculum review before we wrap up Step 1. It requires tremendous effort. Once the process is completed, it's time to share the fruits of your labor in the form of a memo, report, or presentation. For one thing, it is important for the Council to see the finished product. For another, it's important for the broader school community (central administration, faculty and staff, parents, and students) to know about the changes. But watch the protocol. Remember what I said in the introduction about the "conceptual." Odds are that the recommendations are just that, *recommendations*—and must get the blessings of central office and/or the board of education before they can be implemented. You may be sent back to the drawing board: "Too much of this. . . . Not enough of that." It's a good thing you didn't go public. If that's the case (and it probably is), the summary must have limited distribution. The memo details *proposed* changes—I emphasize *proposed*. Be careful *who* gets this information, and in what *order* they get it. Cabinet? Full faculty (via memo or at a meeting)? PTA? Scheduling Committee? Superintendent? Board of Education? In what order is this information shared?[5] Here, for example, are excerpts from a Curriculum Review Council's final report enumerating proposed changes in Math:

---

1. As planned, Sequential Math 3 will be phased out, thereby completing the conversion to the state's new "Math A" and "Math B" curriculum. We will no longer have to run the confusing two-tier system.

2. The Statistics elective, run for the first time this past year, has been very successful, so much so that we are exploring the possibility of converting it to an AP course.

3. Math 1A classes will be regrouped at midyear based on ability. Those struggling most will be identified and put in a separate section for the second semester.

4. Computer Programming 3 and AP Computer will be combined, with the students given the option of taking the AP exam. Neither draws enough students separately, so it makes sense to combine them from the beginning. Also, the course descriptions for both are being rewritten to reflect new computer languages being taught.

Summary

Step 1 is the curriculum review process—adding, deleting, modifying. It's analogous to opening a new restaurant and preparing the menu. For an established school, it entails the formation of a Curriculum Review Council (principal's cabinet or scheduling committee) that will go through this exercise every year. The procedures and criteria for making those decisions were enumerated.

---

[5] Early in my scheduling career, information about a proposed course change leaked out to the parents. A few days later, one of the PTA leaders ran into a board member in the frozen foods aisle at the local supermarket. She congratulated him on the board's decision to add this much-needed course to the curriculum. Apparently, the board member knew nothing about it. Smoke was coming out of his ears when he called me about this lapse in communication. He was furious about being the last to know about the proposed change—and for good reason.

TASKS FOR STEP 1

A total curriculum review: Add . . . Drop . . . Modify.

- Who does it?
- How is it done?
- When is it done?
- To whom is the report distributed?

Step 2

Package It

Four Steps for Preparing the Scheduling Materials

The menu is ready and it's *almost* time to take orders. First, though, we must *package* this information so that our customers (the students) will make wise decisions. There are *four* distinct parts to this step: *course codes, course titles, course descriptions,* and *the course catalogue.* These backstage preparations must be carefully choreographed before the curtain goes up on the scheduling process itself. Otherwise, huge problems loom. Students and parents need complete and accurate information to make the best-informed choices, which will impact on data collection in the next step.

Nomenclature

This is a fancy word for "course codes." Errors made now can prove *extremely* costly later. You need a logical coding system, one not prone to mistakes.

If you are satisfied with your set of codes, you can skip this step. However, if you are starting from scratch or want to avoid some of the pitfalls that your established codes may be causing, read this section carefully. Your set of course codes is your "shorthand." Not only will there be thousands of them—but they will be used for scheduling, report cards, and student transcripts. Furthermore, they will be handled by counselors, teachers, secretaries, aides, and data entry operators.

How are we going to label our courses? Let's return to the earlier example in which we listed alternatives in math instruction for ninth graders. In a one-room school house, "Math" would do the trick, but it certainly would not provide enough information in a large school like USA High School, because a large school's course codes need to contain more information about the course. In its course codes, you would need to know information as to the *type* of course, *grade* level, and even the *ability* level. Math 2 . . . Math 2H . . . MA1201—just to give a few examples of what's out there.

Whatever you decide, just make sure the coding system is clear and consistent. Mistakes made here will be felt up and down the line. Suppose you have a student body of 1,200 students, each signing up for seven subjects + lunch. For the moment, we will omit half-year courses and alternative choices, which will have to be listed as well and will increase that number. At the very minimum, then: $1,200 \times 8 = 9,600$ codes.

That's great deal of information to be entered into the system, and we've only just begun. Then will follow changes to the students' original choices, adjustments based on canceled classes, schedule changes once the school year begins, entries on report cards several times a year, and ultimately a permanent record card (aka transcript or academic history). Ergo, a logical, consistent system of course codes is critical.

Let's take a look at what *not* to do. What's wrong with the following codes?

EZ5   SC01   WJ172

For starters, the three codes are different in length. The first is three characters, the second is four, and the third is five characters in length. Whoever is doing the data entry is not going to know what to expect for each entry—and mistakes will proliferate. Select one model and stick with it. As we shall see below, the number of characters depends on the amount of information you wish encoded and will be a function of the size of your school and the depth and breadth of your course offerings.

Second, the codes mix and match numbers and letters. I suggest that this *is* a good idea—but not the way it's done here. Take a look at the three examples above. In the second, is the "O" a zero or the letter "O"; in the third, is the "1" a number or a letter? If it's a letter, is it a capital "I" or a small "l"? They look similar, don't they?

Third, since there is no pattern to the formation of the codes, there may be some confusion as to the characters themselves. For example, there may be mix-ups between a "Z" and a "2" . . . a "5" and an "S" . . . and an "I" and a "1." The handwriting of many of our best educators resembles what a doctor scribbles on a prescription pad.[1]

Little mistakes now will cause huge headaches down the road because you will end up with inaccurate data once the decision-making process begins. Again, you may be satisfied with your existing code system. Just be aware of some of the alternatives out there that minimize the chances for clerical errors.

Example 1. Take a look at these course codes: 4310, 7153, 8201. According to this system, all courses are assigned a four-digit code. Each digit stands for something: the first indicates the *department,* the second indicates the course's *duration* (1 = fall, 2 = spring, and 3 = full year), and the last two tell you something about the *course.* For example, 4310 translates to: Math department . . . full-year . . . ninth grade introductory course. This is the code for the mainstream Algebra course for freshmen. Makes sense, right? Similarly, 7153 can be broken down to: Science department . . . fall semester . . . elective 3 taken during the junior year (5th semester). Even with just two examples, you're beginning to catch on. After a while, this system becomes the lingo of the schedulers. *You* may want to build *other* information into your system—such as ability level or makeup of the class.

---

[1]One of the most confusing course codes I've come across was: 501IL. It translated to the laboratory portion of a biology course for Special Ed students. It won the "prize" with the "1IL" as well as the "two-faced" "0" and sometimes-hard-to-read "5." A close runner up was the "WJ172" which reminded me of the call letters of a radio station and was prone to errors with the "J," the "1," the "7," and the "2."

Example 2. Which telephone number is easier to remember: BU8–2420 or 282–2420? A combination of letters and numbers is not only easier to remember, but also less prone to mistakes. This principle applies to the creation of course codes as well. The following four-character alphanumeric code was used in the New York City schools for quite a while. It worked because it made sense and contained a great deal of information:

Department	Subject	Level	Code

To illustrate: What does the code HA12 stand for?

> **H** = History department, **A** = American, **1** = first semester, **2** = two-term sequence

Actually, just three characters work: HA1. The fourth character is an optional code that can be used in any way. For example, it might signify something about the class itself. Here are some of the optional codes to consider. Note: These are suggestions only; make the system work for you:

- 3 = alternative school
- 5 = general/skills track
- 6 = ESL
- 7 = college prep/academic
- 8 = special education
- 9 = honors

Under this system, HA13, HA17, and HA19 are all the first semester of an American history course; the first is for students in a school-within-a-school setup[2]; the second is for students in the regular academic program; the last is for honors students. Makes sense. Should this information be included in the course title as well? We'll deal with that sensitive question below.

Recap

Designing course codes is hardly the most exciting part of the job, but a well-thought-out system will reap the dividends of quicker data entry, fewer mistakes, and a shorthand readily understandable to all participants.

Course Titles

Course *titles* are just as important as course *codes*. Once again, they appear in course catalogues, on student schedules, on report cards, and ultimately on the permanent record. Note the word *permanent*. The academic history will remain long after you've

---

[2]Alternative schools (a.k.a. schools within schools) seem to be proliferating. Although there are many types, the three most common are: (1) programs for at-risk youngsters; (2) academies for the gifted; (3) house arrangements whereby large schools are broken down into smaller units or communities.

departed the scene. Don't let your legacy be cute, confusing titles that are meaningful only to you and your colleagues, in-jokes nobody else understands.

An illustration is worth a thousand words. When evaluating student transcripts, the NCAA questioned the validity of a math course. "Mickey Mouse Math" had been served up as an alternative to juniors and seniors who wanted to take an additional nonsequential math course. This title did not sit well with the authorities. In cases like this one, the home high school is contacted and a full course description must follow, detailing exactly what this course purports to cover to make sure that it is up to snuff. Imagine, also, how a prospective employer would react to such a course title. While it is certainly not the fault of the applicant, it is not going to shed favorable light on him.

I have encountered one controversy with regard to course codes. In an alternative school for at-risk students, the faculty objected to the word *alternative* in the course title itself. For example, "Global History—Alternative." After much internal debate, a compromise was struck whereby it was ultimately decided to drop the word *alternative* from the title, but this course was given a separate course *code*. Rules for course titles for Special Ed courses vary from state to state and must be checked.

Recap

Don't be overly creative with course titles. Get to the point: "Freshman Writing Seminar," "Math 2 Honors," "Current Events," "Conversational French."

Course Descriptions

With course codes and titles in place, you're ready for the third part of this step: course descriptions. Once again, proper planning at this stage can go a long way in preventing problems down the line. Of the four substeps, this is the most important.

Returning to our restaurant analogy, you want customers to know enough about the menu items without having to ask too many questions. All they really need to know should be clearly stated on the menu. On the one hand, you don't want to bore the customer with too much detail. It shouldn't read like the telephone book, with nothing more than one wordy description after another that few parents and students are going to want to read. At the other extreme, you want to avoid descriptions that are so brief they omit pertinent information. Walk a very narrow line and include the minimum essentials that students (and their parents) need to know.

As a rookie English teacher, I was permitted to offer a new elective called Mass Media. Imagine my elation when I found out that so many students had signed up that there would be five sections. Well, that ego-booster was quickly deflated after the first day of school when I gave out the course outline listing all the requirements. The students had signed up in droves, thinking that they were going to be watching television. This mass preregistration had nothing to do with me or the course itself. Little did they know they would have four projects to complete as well as two big exams to take. There was a mad dash to the guidance counselors' offices—and a mass exodus from my classes. It was quite a learning experience, and a humbling one at that.

For the next school year, my supervisor helped me construct the following course description, which made the expectations for this elective abundantly clear. I ended up with only two sections, which was fine. At least all of the students came into my class knowing what they had gotten themselves into.

A good description is about seventy-five words in length and must include *eight* parts. Read the sample (from my Mass Media elective) and try to identify them before you look at the legend below. You need to understand the eight parts and the purpose of each.

Mass Media (E503). A survey course touching briefly on each of the following topics: history of radio and television, principles of journalism, elements of television and radio production, directing, scriptwriting, educational television, advertising, broadcast journalism, and children's programming. Requirements include: two full-length scripts, one audience measurement project, and one research paper. Offered: fall term only. Credited: for elective credit *only.* Minimum grade of B and recommendation from teacher in previous English class required.

---

1. Course Title. The importance of having an appropriate course title was detailed above.

2. Course Code. Ditto for the course code. But don't forget to include this short-hand symbol in the catalogue so that when the students begin to sign up, they will be signing up for the right thing. Titles don't always translate to correct codes when students actually sit down to preregister.

3. Brief Narrative Description. They need to know what to expect. Is this a lecture course? Seminar? Lab? Performance class? Something else?

4. Sample Topics. Students need to know what material they will be covering. In the case at hand, the course title Mass Media simply didn't tell enough.

5. Requirements. Absolutely *critical* for avoiding future misunderstandings. Once again, in the example being used, if the students had been aware during the preregistration process as to the demands of this course, many wouldn't have signed up. The course description lets the students know the volume of work.[3]

√ Helpful Hint 5

Can a school require students to take Advanced Placement (AP) exams (assuming funds are provided for those who have legitimate financial need)? Definitely—as long as it is stipulated in the course description. Several districts were having problems with top-flight students' coming down with premature bouts of "senioritis" after getting their college acceptances in the fall. They practically tuned out their AP courses, which in some cases had been their ticket of admission. Needless to say, this infuriated the faculty. When it came to the AP test itself, some didn't bother to show up. The following year, those districts indicated (in the course catalogue) that "taking the Advanced Placement exam is a course requirement; it serves as the final exam. Failure to take the test will result in a 'zero' for the final exam and be factored into the final grade."

---

[3]When we get to Step #4, we will encounter similar examples when students mistakenly sign up for Advanced Placement European Studies—not fully understanding what they have gotten themselves into.

6. When Offered. When program planning[4] takes place, students need to know when during the year the course is offered, particularly if it is a required class or one that will complete a sequence. A senior came to the second semester and realized the only Home Economics course she could take to complete a three-year sequence was offered only in the fall. Of course, her guidance counselor shouldered some of this responsibility. You can see why this information must be included in the description.

7. Course Credit. "The Mass Media class may be used for *elective credit only.* Although it is offered by the English Department, it may *not* be taken in lieu of a required English class." Refer back to that earlier discussion about the three meanings of the term *elective* presented in the Introduction. Once again, we don't want a senior to discover that he is a course short of meeting the graduation requirements.

8. Eligibility. This is a particularly thorny issue with regard to honors, college-level, and AP courses. The jury is still out. Should admission be based on self-selection or past performance? It's a heated debate in many districts, but not our concern here. What *is* our concern is that the policy needs to be clearly stated so that there is no possible misunderstanding. As a principal, I had numerous parent conferences about this contentious issue: namely, asking for exceptions to place students in honors and AP courses when they hadn't been recommended for them.

My workshop participants often suggest the following compromise: "Admit anyone into that higher level class on a trial basis—but if it turns out to be too challenging, allow the student to drop down a level after the first grading period." This proposal sounds good, but as we shall see in Step 4, it's not practical. I call it double dipping. You're having the student make a reservation in *two* places, not good practice moneywise. In the ideal world, I would agree to it in a heartbeat, but not these days. Much more on the dollars 'n' cents of the decision-making process will follow. To continue our restaurant analogy, you're allowing the customer to order two dishes, sample both, keep one, and send the other back. Cannot do! A good course description coupled with clearly spelled-out eligibility requirements obviates this problem.

Recap

If you don't have a set of course descriptions, you face an arduous task the first time around. If you methodically break down the huge task by involving all the department heads (as well as some administrative interns), the job will get done. Just leave adequate time to do it. Once it's in place, all you will need to do is yearly tune-ups. Go back to Step 1: Add . . . Drop . . . Modify. Confusion, needless questions, and most important of all—massive schedule changes—can be avoided if the students know what to expect.

Course Catalogue

Take a look at the course-offering booklets of the high schools in your area. The amount budgeted will vary from school to school. Some will be slick, professionally

---

[4]The terms "preregistration," "program planning," and "course signs-ups" are used interchangeably.

produced publications, rivaling the fanciest college catalogues, with impressive covers, professional photography, and color graphics, all printed on glossy paper. Others will have been inexpensively printed on newspaper stock with no pictures or illustrations of any kind; they look like telephone directories. Then there are some districts that don't have a course description booklet at all.

Let me state categorically: You need a *dynamite course catalogue,* but it doesn't have to cost a fortune. Here are a number of budget-savers to get the job done within your means. First, the pages can be typed and edited in-house. Second, they can be reproduced on your own photocopy machine. Third, an attractive cover can be designed. Fourth, it can be printed on inexpensive card stock. Fifth, photography, illustrations, and other graphics can be provided by students. More on course catalogues in Step 3.

Consider including a flowchart for each department, outlining the required courses, ability levels within each, and additional electives (if any). Again, see Step 3 for an example. Departments that are all-elective in makeup could add illustrations.

√ Helpful Hint 6

You can turn to your Fine Arts Department and run a contest for an attention-grabbing cover. Students will jump at the chance to be the winner, not so much for the prize you might offer, but for the recognition and to be able to say that their art was used on the cover of a school publication. No doubt that they will add it to their portfolios and share it with college admissions officials when the time comes. I've seen some beautiful pen-and-ink drawings and clever cartoons on high school course catalogue covers. If your district has a Graphic Arts/Technology program, you can assign the entire project to the advanced students. The aforementioned cartoons, flowcharts, and graphics could also be produced by the students, thereby showcasing their talents.

In addition to the course listings, the catalogue can include other important information: a roster of faculty and staff, graduation requirements, extracurricular programs, a calendar of events, and so on. Some schools view the catalogue as their premier public relations document and will use its captive audience to promulgate everything from the school's philosophy and policies to its rules and regulations. Others take a more bare-bones approach and stick to the course descriptions themselves.[5]

Summary

Each of the ten scheduling steps has its own character. Step 2 requires detail work. As soon as Step 1 (Planning) is complete, work must begin on Step 2 (Packaging). Generally this work takes place during December. Although the master scheduler is ultimately responsible for its successful completion, this work can be delegated to an

---

[5]As educators, we've all experienced the "Eureka!" phenomenon when one of our students "gets it." After completing the second step and underscoring the need for a dynamite course catalogue, one participant told me that his district had no such document. Six months later he sent me a copy of the first edition of his high school's course catalogue. It was inexpensively produced (using student input)—yet highly professional in appearance.

assistant principal, guidance counselor, administrative intern, or members of the scheduling committee. Nevertheless, there must be ownership by each person who assumes responsibility for one of the substeps. We will see down the road what major problems will result if proper care and attention are not given to these preparations. Course codes, titles, descriptions, and catalogues must be carefully thought out; otherwise, there will be a big price to pay in later steps.

TASKS FOR STEP 2

The four tasks associated with this step are very concrete:

- Develop a consistent and functional set of *course codes*.
- Review all the *course titles* to make sure that they make sense.
- Write *course descriptions* for each and every course, making sure that they all contain the eight parts described above.
- Publish a dynamite *course catalogue*. It need not be expensive and should use student contributions as much as possible.

Step 3

Market It

Reaching Out to Students and Parents

The curriculum is set, courses have been titled and coded, course descriptions have been written, and a course catalogue has been published. The next step is to *market* your product to your consumers, that is, the students and their parents. So far, all of your work has been behind the scenes. No longer. In this step, you will be meeting your public. As noted above, planning takes place in October and early November, and packaging takes place in December. The marketing phase occurs in January.

The information will flow two ways: First, it will go from the school to the students and their parents; second, data will be collected from the students and their parents and be delivered to the school.

Disseminating Information

Six methods for disseminating information will be presented. Choose a single alternative or a combination of two or more. There is no one right way. Whatever works, given your circumstances, population, and budget, is the best method.

Before we turn to the marketing techniques, let's return to the course catalogue and create some excitement for the step to follow. How do you generate interest and excitement among students and parents? How do you hype the scheduling process?

We'll take a lesson from one of our most popular publications, *TV Guide.* Which issue produces the highest circulation? No doubt about it: the fall preview, which comes out every September. This eagerly awaited edition hypes the upcoming season, highlights the new shows, and tells the viewers what to expect. Your school catalogue should do precisely the same things. The key difference is that yours comes out in January and previews the scheduling season. And, like *TV Guide,* it hypes the upcoming [scheduling] season, highlights the new courses, and tells students and their parents what to expect. Use your catalogue to generate the same excitement as the scheduling process gets underway. Here is a list of features you should include:

- An attention-grabbing cover (selected from a student competition)
- An attractive layout, with a separate section for each department
- Carefully placed graphics to break up the text
- A flowchart of required/elective courses for each department (sample below)
- An introduction to the scheduling process, including a timeline
- A summary of some of the changes, best written by the principal
- The word *New!* appropriately placed next to the first-time offerings
- The word *Changed!* placed next to those that have been modified
- The course selection contract (to be explained below)

English Department Offerings

9th grade:	Standard introductory course offered on three different levels: Honors, Regular, or Skills
10th grade:	Choice of *writing* elective one semester and *reading* elective the *other semester*
11th grade:	Preparatory course for State Standards Exam and SAT taught on three different levels
12th grade:	Advanced Placement, Senior Comp. & Literature, or choice of two electives on approved list
For elective credit only:	Half-year courses: Dramatics, Journalism, Creative Writing, Public Speaking

---

Now, we're ready to take a look at some of the specific ways to go public.

1. Curriculum Fair

Highly recommended! As the scheduling cycle kicks off, this evening program is not only a way to stir up some excitement, but also engages the students and their parents in the process immediately.

- Select well in advance an evening in January. Try to avoid a scheduling conflict with any other major event (concert, board of education meeting, etc.).
- Make sure that the date appears on the district calendar.
- Send a flyer out to all parents two weeks in advance.
- If your school has a good Web site, post an announcement there as well.
- Ask your PTA to get the word out on its network.
- Submit a press release to the local newspaper(s) and radio/TV stations.
- Send an emissary to the feeder junior high/middle school(s). A large segment of your audience will consist of incoming eighth-becoming-ninth graders.[1]

---

[1]Schools tend to wrestle with identifying grade levels. In other words, when we say "ninth graders," are we referring to current students or next year's class? I use the expression "eighth becoming ninth graders" or "8 to 9's" to avoid confusion. Choose whatever works for you; but keep in mind that you will have problems down the road if you don't get your grade levels straight, especially when the numbers start coming in.

- Have guidance counselors reach out to their counselees.
- As the date draws closer, spread the word via public address announcements.
- Stress the importance of the schedule-building process in all communications.

The curriculum fair itself should be divided into three parts. For the first half hour (maximum), all students and parents should attend a large-group meeting at which there is a brief keynote address by the principal to kick off the process, followed by a presentation from the guidance department touching upon the graduation requirements and an overview of "what's new" for the upcoming year. Keep in mind that for your incoming freshmen, this might be their very first exposure to the high school.

Following the large-group meeting, the students and their parents should then be divided into four grade-level meetings (ninth, tenth, eleventh, and twelfth) where course catalogues and programming planning worksheets are given out. Once again, when I say ninth graders, I am referring to current eighth graders (next year's ninth graders). The same holds true for tenth, eleventh, and twelfth graders. Attendance understandably declines for upperclassmen (tenth into eleventh grade and eleventh into twelfth). Current seniors don't have to attend.

The guidance staff and administrators are paired to cover the four meetings. Major additions, deletions, and changes in the course of study are highlighted. If possible, a summary sheet is prepared for each grade. The students and the parents are walked through the scheduling process, department by department, step by step. Adequate time should be reserved for questions. This part of the program should last about forty-five minutes, but certainly not longer than an hour. Any more time is overkill.

The third leg of the curriculum fair consists of tables set up in the cafeteria or some other commons area. There should be one for each department. At a given signal or agreed-upon time, all students and parents converge on the fair itself where representatives from each department (the department head plus one, two, or more teachers) are available to answer questions. Students and parents, particularly incoming ninth graders, are most interested in meeting the staff. Equipment, posters, books, handouts, and the like should be set up for each table's display. Some departments will need electricity to power their displays, so have a few extra power strips on hand.

2. Parent Meetings

If you don't want to do anything as elaborate as a curriculum fair, then more streamlined parent meetings will suffice. Separate sessions for incoming students, transfer students, and Special Education pupils are especially important. Ever-changing course requirements, state mandates, curricula, and new programs can be very confusing. An evening program titled "Everything You Wanted to Know About Program Planning" will be well received. At the very least, ask for some time every year at a regularly scheduled PTA meeting. Just realize that you would then have a limited audience.

In the case of our brand new USA High School, this step would entail meetings for all parents. They should be scheduled at different times (before school, during school, after school, and evenings) to accommodate working parents. For established schools, it means meeting with parents of students coming from incoming feeder schools, mostly current eighth graders. For junior high and middle schools, there could be separate parent meetings at each of the feeder elementary schools.

√ Helpful Hint 7

Consult your PTA. Its leaders probably will be thrilled to help organize and publicize these meetings. You may even choose to let them cosponsor the event. Along these lines, for schools with a high degree of student mobility, new-parent meetings for transfer students as well as other new admits would definitely be well received.

Course selection is a highly complex process demanding many decisions. Parents want to be informed as to the options open to their children as well as the process itself. It is crucial that they be kept in the loop in order to avoid costly mistakes later on.

3. Large-Group Assemblies

You know your customers; you know what will work and what won't. Some schools bring together the entire student body to explain the program planning process in a single session. Supervision is the key to success in this setting. Classes must be seated intact, and teachers must actively supervise. Zone defense, so to speak. Administrators, guidance staff, and teachers must make sure that students are attentive. This plan might work in a middle-sized school with a separate assembly for each grade level. However, it might prove impractical in a large high school with several thousand students, unless, of course, you are willing to repeat the program several times.

4. Extended Homerooms

Once upon a time there was a homeroom period in every secondary school; the "official class" was where attendance was taken. Some have abolished this artificial arrangement and have attendance taken in subject classes. If your school has a homeroom period, you may do much of the paper and pencil work for program planning there. Whether teacher-directed or via the public address system with homeroom teacher assistance, the job can get done. You may encounter resistance from subject class teachers who resent doing administrative/guidance work at the expense of instructional time. Nor are they invested in their homeroom students as much as they are in their subject class pupils. While some preliminary work can be done, it isn't the best method.

√ Helpful Hint 8

The next generation of homeroom is the "advisory period," in which teachers have a chance to meet with an assigned group of students on an occasional basis. Its purpose is to promote increased interaction between faculty and students. In places where it does exist, it might be the perfect setting for program planning.

---

5. Group Guidance

If a large-group assembly or a homeroom period is not appropriate, then subject classes can be grouped together for the same purpose. Suppose you want to meet with "juniors only" to explain electives and special programs available in the twelfth grade. Consider grouping together all first period eleventh grade English (or Social Studies) classes for a presentation by the Guidance Department. The size of the school will determine how many sections per period. The process is repeated for each period. By the end of the day, all students in the grade have heard the presentation, in groups no larger than 50. In a large school with multiple sections, you may have to schedule more than one presentation per period. (Subject teachers should remain to assist with supervision.) Group guidance works well at the junior high/middle school level also.

Select a subject that all students take, such as English or Social Studies. You will quickly learn that they are frequently targeted for special presentations. Every effort should be made to rotate such infringements on instructional time among all the subject areas so no one takes the full brunt.[2]

6. Individual Conferences

Obviously ideal is the individual conference during which the counselor meets with the student (and sometimes his parents) to develop next year's course of study. Of course, the feasibility of this approach depends on the counselor-to-student ratio. In many schools, guidance counselors are carrying case loads of several hundred students, so it is just not possible to have an individual sit-down with each and every one of the students. Even if counselors spend just ten minutes with each of their counselees, they will not be able to reach all of their students during the allotted time.

> ### √ Helpful Hint 9
>
> A compromise is to have the counselor meet with several students at a time. In addition to making sense timewise, this approach has a fringe benefit: During the discussion, the students can learn from one another. They can get valuable insights from their classmates. I recall eavesdropping on such a meeting at which three students were offering their advice as to which was the best elective for a classmate to take, given her intended major. Some guidance counselors actually prefer this interaction, possible when they meet with several students at a time rather than just one.

7. Mailings

There are schools that complete the entire program planning process by mail. The student and parent receive the course catalogue delivered to the home, a detailed set of instructions is included, and a form (see the next section) for indicating course choices is also included. Sometimes the back cover of the course catalogue is used for this purpose. There is little or no personal contact between the school and the home unless a specific question must be answered or more information is needed. Efficient? Yes. Effective? Draw your own conclusions as to what is lost with this method.

---

[2]As a rookie building administrator, I was accosted by a senior English teacher at the end of the year with a list of all the times her class had been used for guidance, assemblies, drills, surveys, and special presentations. She had lost more than ten instructional periods over the course of the year. It was an eye-opener.

8. Online

Some schools are now pioneering the world of cyberspace when it comes to program planning. You can order bridal gifts, groceries, and clothing online. Now you can indicate your course requests in the same way. I still prefer personal interaction with give-and-take that is part 'n' parcel of some of the other methods. Still, this is an option from which you can choose. Perhaps online preregistration can be the final step after one of the other methods incorporating informational sessions is used.

Recap

Eight methods have been presented for disseminating scheduling information to students and their parents. As stated at the outset, this is a marketing function. Depending on your school's culture and resources, select one or a combination of these to deliver the program planning information your "customers" need.

Over the years, I've taken my share of kidding about hyping the scheduling process. I plead guilty and stand by that belief. In my travels, I have seen schools in which scheduling (and the course selection process in particular) is a low priority and treated as a necessary evil. Unfortunately, the end result reflects that disdain. I hold to my statement that you need to create some excitement about the process. After all, what should be more important to the faculty and students than the courses they teach and take? Now, we're ready for information to flow in the other direction.

Gathering Data

So far, the information has gone in one direction: from the school to the students and parents. Now it's time to gather data as the communication becomes a two-way street. The options have been presented. The students have made their choices, and now it is time to make their selections. To continue our analogy: The restaurant has been built, the menus have been given out, and now it's time to take orders.

Here is a compendium of possibilities. Your choice will depend on your circumstances. Pay close attention to the final alternative, which will be presented as a Helpful Hint. As far as I'm concerned, it is one of the most valuable tips in the book.

Before we look at the list, we need to say something about timing. As noted, Step 3, Market It, takes place in January. There is considerable variation as to when students submit their course requests. I strongly recommend that this process starts in February and continues until mid-March. Some schools complete this step as early as January. Frankly, I believe that this is premature. Assuming that students get report cards at midyear (February 1), those grades provide necessary input to make the most intelligent choices regarding next year's classes. Once report cards are circulated—get ready, get set, go! Use one or more of the methods enumerated to get the job done.

1. Checklists

All of the school's courses and codes are listed on a preprinted sheet. All that the students have to do is circle or check their choices.

2. Bubble Sheets

If your school is tied into a computer/data entry system, then the expectation may be for the course codes to be bubbled in by the student. For example, the code for that Mass Media elective, E615, would be bubbled E–6–1–5. The danger here is that this method is prone to error. If students are not careful and do not bubble correctly, you will end up with dirty data. The computer can't guess what students meant when invalid codes turn up. Remember what we said in Step 2 about bad codes coming back to haunt us down the line. This is just the first example.

3. Fill in the Blanks

The student returns to the guidance department a list of the courses (or codes) he wishes to take. As noted above, this list may be on the inside back cover of the course catalogue. Some schools have a dedicated data entry operator who feeds this information into the computer.

Name (or preprinted label)_____Counselor_____
1_ _ _ _2_ _ _ _3_ _ _ _4_ _ _ _5_ _ _ _6_ _ _ _7_ _ _ _8_ _ _ _

4. Direct Data Entry

Some schools have the counselor enter the course codes as he meets with students. I liken this to a reservations agent booking information online as it comes from the customer. There are two advantages to this method: First, it is immediate. Second, the counselor is probably more adept at making these data entries, so there will be far fewer errors than if the students had bubbled them.

5. Course Selection Contract

This approach is highly recommended. As a matter of fact, it is the basis of one of the most important Helpful Hints. Students preregister in February . . . register for those courses on the opening day of school . . . and complete those courses in a semester or two. How many of the original preregistrants actually end up sticking with their original choices? Guidance counselors will tell you that there is an alarming increase in the number of changes from the course selection process until the first day of classes, let alone until the end of the course. It's a sad commentary, but students tend not to view their choices as commitments; they are very casual about their choices. Sometimes they simply do not give much initial thought to the process, other times they just don't take the process seriously: "Put down anything; you can always change your mind later." I've heard that comment all too many times. They are teenagers. Many of them can't think beyond the end of the day. Suddenly you are asking them to make decisions that will not be implemented for another six months. Little wonder that they give short shrift to their course selections.

√ Helpful Hint 10

How do you convince students—and their parents—that course selections must be taken seriously? They need to be viewed as commitments. A course selection sheet is just not enough. To start to get the point across, I recommend that you call this document the course selection contract.

This, however, is only the beginning. I have played out the following scene scores of times; it was a staple at the annual curriculum fair and repeated at all of the grade-level assemblies devoted to the scheduling process. Bottom line: It works.

I start out by saying that I'm not a mean guy, nor are my fellow administrators a mean group of people. Therefore, everyone has to understand why when we say "No!" to casually changing course selections later in the process that we are not mean. I quickly clarify that there are a few legitimate reasons for course changes and list them: clerical errors, pass-fail reversals, class cancellations, and the like. But, I go on to explain that they are the exception, not the rule. As I continue, I point out that many of those other requests for changes are based purely on whim—and that's something we cannot accept as we start to build the master schedule.

This stern introduction usually engenders silence, which I am prepared for. Now my goal is to win the audience back. To illustrate, I tell the following story: "Have you ever gone to a wedding or a banquet and as you get seated at your table, the server asks you what you would like for your main course: chicken, fish, or roast beef?" At this point, I randomly point to three people in the audience and ask them: "Chicken, fish, or roast beef?" It doesn't matter what they say. Suppose those three people say: "Fish–fish–chicken" (I guess it must be a health-conscious crowd!). Loud and clear, I repeat their answers for everyone to hear: "Fish–fish–chicken."

Then I turn back to the audience: "Probably without too much thought, you would have given your response the same way." I return to the affair: "The party proceeds. The appetizers and salads are served and there is a lot of dancing. About an hour later, the bandleader asks the guests to please return to their tables as he announces: 'Your main course is now being served.' Once seated, a server passes your table with plates of steaming roast beef, delicious end cuts. So much for the healthy choice! You want a piece of that savory red meat as well. However, based on your initial requests—not to mention those of several hundred other guests—the chef spent the past hour preparing the appropriate amount of chicken, fish, and roast beef."

Invariably this scenario evokes considerable laughter. Now I'm ready to deliver the punch line: "Imagine what will happen when you, as well as any number of other guests, have a change of heart. There will be chaos in the kitchen. All that leftover fish, but not enough roast beef to go around."[3]

This role play, presented with a fair amount of histrionics (and even a dance step or two) always generates a great deal of laughter. But it gets the point across. Then comes the zinger: "So it is with course requests. And now, I have to get very serious. (I pause while I wait for the audience to settle down.) Based on the courses you signed up for with your counselor, we have assigned teachers and formed classes. For example, if twenty-five students sign up for a particular class, we will offer one section. If seventy-two students sign up for another course we will probably offer three sections, and if 125 students sign up for yet another course, we'll probably run five sections, given a class size of twenty-five. And so it goes for each one of our several hundred courses. Do you see what a complicated process it is? This is how the master schedule gets built."

By this point, the audience has gotten very quiet again. But I'm still not finished. "Therefore, I tell you this story because we want you to understand that it's not unreasonable for us to say 'no' when students try to change their course requests. You're one person. Imagine if 1,200 [or however many students there are in your

---

[3]I recently went to an affair where the server gave me a ticket that stated what I had chosen for my main course. When that main course was served, I had to produce the ticket "proving" what I had ordered. I have incorporated this anecdote into my "routine."

school] all do the same thing, just with one request, let alone more. To permit whole-sale changes in course requests would obviously cause overcrowding in some courses and imbalances in others. I hope that this illustration gives you an inside look at how building the master schedule works from the inside. To put it another way, we can't afford to run out of roast beef and have all the fish left over and rotting!"

I always conclude the way I started: "Now you can understand that we are not mean when we say 'no' to a request for a change. We want you to be part of the process and to understand why." Does presenting this scenario eliminate requests for course changes? No, but I can tell you after years of building master schedules that it drastically reduces them.

√ Helpful Hint 11

Develop some version of the infamous "chicken–fish–roast beef" story. Not only will it explain the process to students and parents, but it will also get them on your side.

This story has become legend—and it successfully got the point across to generations of students and parents. To begin with, it drastically reduces (although it doesn't eliminate) requests for course request changes. Second, it gets students and parents to take the course selection decision-making process more seriously. Third, and perhaps most important of all, it helps to break down the us-versus-you or administration-versus-student syndrome. It projects the message that we're all in this together.

The Use of Alternates

More schools are making use of alternates when taking course requests. Counselors can record these by hand. Some scheduling software packages have a provision for the alternate course choices to be listed along with the primary selections.

It is important to know a student's alternate course choices for three reasons. First, if his primary choice fails to make the cut-off and is canceled, the counselor can revert to the alternate, which is already on file. In other words, if the student has requested "World Dramatic Literature," but the course doesn't have the enrollment to run, the counselor already knows that this student is willing to take "Mythology" instead. Second, if the alternate course itself is on the cusp of being canceled, perhaps several of the students on the alternate list would consider a switch over so that it could be salvaged. For example, suppose that only eleven students signed up for "Advertising and Design"—but another twenty listed it as an alternate. A few of the twenty might be willing to make the switch to save the course. Third, when we get to actually scheduling the courses in Steps 6, 7, and 8, it might turn out that a course has a conflict with another course (i.e., they both meet only once—and at the same time). Hence, this course may be the one that will be dropped, and the alternate can be substituted.

There is another practical reason for listing alternates when the original course selections are made: Experienced schedulers will tell you that they need this information at their fingertips because it is not always easy to get in touch with the student. Why wait until the very last minute? Have the alternates on file and readily accessible.

Here, for example, are the course selections and alternates for a twelfth grader:

Primary	Alternate
English 12 Advanced Placement	English 12 Honors
Social Studies 12 Honors	Social Studies 12 R
Calculus AB	—
Chemistry—Advanced Placement	Physics—Advanced Placement
Genetics	Forensic Science
Spanish 5	—
Ceramics	Sculpture
Physical Education	—

Summary

In Step 1 you planned and in Step 2 you packaged. Until this point, the information has gone in one direction. In Step 3, the marketing phase, information is coming back to you. After hyping the scheduling process based on the information you presented, students have to make intelligent course selections. We looked at some methods for disseminating information as well as collecting data. The course selection contract is promoted as a way of getting students to take this process seriously.

TASKS FOR STEP 3

- How are you going to hype the scheduling process about to begin?
- How are you going to disseminate the information to students and parents?
- How and when are you going to collect the data?
- Are you going to record both primary and alternate requests?
- How are you going to underscore the importance of this decision-making process?

Step 4

Count 'Em Up

Determining Tallies, Sections, and Staff

While all ten steps are important, this one is not only particularly critical, but also highly complex. It has been broken down into many small and easy-to-digest ministeps, all with concrete examples, as well as sample forms adaptable for your school.

The Master Tally

I've already recommended that students make their course selections between early February and mid-March. Let's assume the process is completed by March 17. We're going to give St. Patrick's Day a second significance: Tally Day—when the computer generates two critical documents. (We'll get to the second in Step 5.) Right now, we're concerned with the *master tally*, a list of all the courses the school would like to be offering next year and the number of students who have signed up for those courses based on the preregistration process just completed. For example: English 9 = 150, English 9 Honors = 23, Journalism = 17, and so on. Some of those proposed courses won't survive because of low enrollments. To repeat: The master tally lists all the courses and the number of students who have signed to take them.

The master scheduler now faces one of the most daunting parts of the job: going through the master tally to determine the number of sections for each course. Before beginning, you must decide who is delegated this responsibility. Candidates include the principal, assistant principal, and guidance director. These decisions are made in consultation with the department heads. There is no one right person or persons.

Givens

To undertake this budget exercise, we are going to need to do some math. We'll start on the supply side: teachers.

Generally speaking, secondary school teachers teach five classes. As previously mentioned, there are exceptions: In some districts, teachers have only four classes . . . while in some others they have six. It really doesn't matter; it is only a number used for illustrative purposes. If teachers in your district teach a different number, just tailor the exercise to make it fit for you. We'll use five since it fits the vast majority of cases.

Hence, staffing is measured in terms of fifths. A part-time teacher with just one class is "one fifth." Another part-timer, assigned three classes, is "three fifths." A teacher who has five classes (five fifths) is, therefore, full-time.

What about science teachers? In some districts they teach additional periods, and their lab assignments have to be considered above and beyond their classes. There are many arrangements. The principle is the same, but the math is more complicated.

• Science teachers teach only three classes—but each of those classes has an alternate day lab; therefore they have 4.5 classes ($3 \times 1.5 = 4.5$). To bring their teaching load to full complement, they may be assigned Special Education class labs or extra help sessions to make up that extra half class.

• Science teachers teach two lab classes (again, with alternate day labs) and two nonlab classes (such as electives). Hence, their load is $2 \times 1.5 = 3 + 2 = 5$.

Some colleagues prefer to refer to teachers in terms of decimals: a teacher teaching two classes is a .4; another teacher teaching four classes is a .8. Personally, I find decimals a bit more confusing (2 = .4) and prefer to work in fifths (2 = 2). Choose what works best for you; just be consistent so that everyone on the scheduling team speaks the same language. Imagine the confusion, not to mention the mistakes, when one administrator is talking in fifths and the other is talking in decimals.

Determining Teacher Loads

Earlier we said that we would use "30" as our typical class size. It is a nice round number and seems to be typical. Use whatever the average is in your district. Suppose that 150 students sign up for Spanish 3. Given thirty students per class, you divide the 150 by 30—and end up with five sections. Since we also said that a typical teacher teaches five sections, the staffing for Spanish 3 would be "one" teacher. Many districts discuss staffing in terms of FTEs (Full Time Equivalents). In this example, the staffing need for Spanish 3 would be 1 FTE. That doesn't necessarily mean one teacher is teaching all five sections. The total of five could be taught by one person or divided up among several.

If every case were so simple, you could close the book right now. Rarely do things run so smoothly. Sections are a precious commodity and must be used very sparingly. Our mantra will be, "Spend sections wisely." I like the word *spend* because it conjures up thoughts of money. You can go to the bank just so many times. Take a look at this list of complicating factors as we approach the staffing budget.

Bad Breaks. With a preregistration figure of thirty-six, you can't get away with one section, but have to run two with only eighteen students each. Small class size—but costly, and eventually it's going to come out of the hide of something else.

Double-Period Classes. Certain courses require two fifths of teacher time, such as a double-period class for marginal math students. Pedagogically, it's a wise idea, but it's costly. You're spending double the number of sections on a single class.

Science Labs. Many districts add one or more lab periods for science classes. An extra period a week . . . every other day . . . or a double period every day. I'm not minimizing the value of more instructional time, but understand the costs when we start spending precious sections.

Special Education. These classes tend to be far smaller in size. Some will require two teachers being assigned to a single section. For example, a life skills class for the most challenged youngsters may have an extremely low professional-to-student ratio. Probably mandated, pedagogically wise . . . but also expensive. In many states, local, state, or federal funding is available for Special Education programs.

Remedial Classes. Ditto for extra-help classes for marginal students. Certainly a wise idea, but they're going to cost you. Be aware of grants available for youth-at-risk.

Hands-On Classes. It's just not wise to assign thirty students to practical arts, fine arts, and technology classes. One of my strangest memories is an "Introduction to Tech" course in which the students designed their own projects. It was several weeks into the year before the teacher discovered that one group was designing an electric chair. Safety, then, is clearly a factor. Chemistry was always of particular concern to me; a teacher's supervision can go just so far with all those potentially explosive chemicals around. When deciding how many sections to run, I kept Chemistry classes on the smaller side.

Equipment/Stations. The number of computers, lab stations, clarinets, or easels may dictate the maximum class size in keyboarding, chemistry, music, and painting classes, respectively. I've also come across schools in which the size of the standard classrooms dictates the maximum size of the sections—possibly by design.

State Mandates/Requirements/Sequence Issues. You may be ready to cancel an elective with a low preregistration figure—only to discover it's the only course that fulfills a mandated credit or sequence for graduation. Once, I pared down the number of sections by cutting three low-enrollment Home Economics courses. When word got out, I was met by the guidance counselors who informed me that their students were counting on these courses to complete specific graduation requirements. Tail between my legs, I had to restore those sections and cut someplace else. Costly, but I had no choice.

The All-Important Equation

I've already alluded to the fact that sections are precious. No surprise. Staffing is expensive. Before proceeding, you need to understand this simple relationship.

> **TALLIES *turn into* SECTIONS . . .**
> *and*
> **SECTIONS *turn into* STAFF.**

Tallies refer to the number of students signing up for a particular course. Remember the figures for Spanish 3 used above? There were 150 tallies; given thirty students per class, that meant five sections; five sections required one teacher. Let this simple equation be etched on your brain.

Teaching "Demand" and Teaching "Supply"

Think back to your basic Economics course and the fundamental principle of supply and demand. As we shall see, it fully applies to school scheduling.

Teaching demand is the total number of sections needed for all departments. Let's go back yet again to that Spanish 3 example in which we came up with five sections. You would do the calculations for Spanish 1, Spanish 2, Spanish 4, French 1, French 2, and so on. In other words, you would look at the tallies and calculate the number of sections needed for all Language courses. You'd do precisely the same thing for all the other courses in all the other departments: English, Math, Science, Music, Business Education, Physical Education, and all the others. Finally, you would add up all the department subtotals, and your grand total (for all the departments) would be your teaching demand.

But that's only half the story. We have to look at the other side of this equation, too. We need to define teaching supply: your staffing allocation. Your teaching supply is the number of teachers allotted multiplied by five. (Remember, we're using five classes per teacher; substitute any other number to fit if your particular situation.) Don't worry about Science teachers with those pesky labs or part-time teachers who carry less than a full load. They just require more math and we'll deal with them later. Again, simply stated, your teaching need is the number of teachers you have been budgeted multiplied by five. Let's try a few simple examples to calculate teaching capacity:

- 10 FTE teachers = 50 sections (10×5)
- 25 FTE teachers = 125 sections (25×5)
- 40 FTE teachers = 200 sections (40×5)
- 124.4 FTE teachers = 622 sections (124 teachers are teaching 5 classes: $124 \times 5 = 620 +$ an additional $.4 = 2$ more sections, for a total of 622)

To further explain the concept of FTE, a picture is worth a thousand words. The following example will clarify this concept. Look at the following list of teachers in the Math Department at USA High School.

Able	Davis	Gold
Baker	Evers	Harris
Cane	Fox	

It would appear that there are eight teachers in the department. Yes, there are eight members of the department, but the FTE is altogether different. Take a look:

Able	full-time	teaches 5 sections
Baker	part-time dean	teaches only 3 sections
Cane	full-time	teaches 5 sections
Davis	lead teacher/chair	teaches only 2 sections
Evers	full-time	teaches 5 sections
Fox	attendance coordinator	teaches only 4 sections
Gold	full-time	teaches 5 sections
Harris	part-time/shared	teaches only 1 section

Add 'em up: The total is thirty sections. Thirty divided by five equals six. The FTE for the Math Department is six—not eight. Once again, there are eight department members, but staff is not always the same as FTE, as in the case at point.

How to Reconcile Teaching "Demand" and Teaching "Supply"

Now push comes to shove. You're ready to prepare the staffing budget for your school. Follow this eight-step procedure.

1. Generate the master tally as soon as the course selection process is complete; mid-March was suggested as a benchmark time.

2. Go department by department.

3. Look at the tallies for each individual course.

4. Determine the number of sections you need to run for each course; at the same time ascertain which courses will be canceled because of low enrollment. Make sure you notify the Guidance Department so that student programs can be adjusted, probably with the use of alternates, as explained above.

5. Add up the number of sections needed for all courses in each department.

6. Calculate the number of sections you need for all departments.

7. Put that number up against the teaching supply you have been given.

8. Determine whether you can run your instructional program (teaching demand) given the staffing allocation (teaching supply) you've been budgeted.

Example

To illustrate, let's try this very simple example.

- You analyze the tallies and come up with a teaching demand of 165 sections.
- You are informed that your staffing budget (teaching supply) is 29.4.
- Do you have enough staff to run this program? No!
- Divide 165 by 5; that number of sections requires 33 teachers ($165/5 = 33$).
- You've been given only 29.4 staff members; you're very short.
- Of course, an alternative way to do the figuring is to multiply the 29.4 by 5 ($29.4 \times 5 = 147$). The conclusion is the same: Your teaching capacity is 147; you don't have enough staff to cover the teaching needs of 165 sections.

Recap

Up to this point we have discussed staffing (FTEs, fifths, decimals, etc.). We have seen how tallies translate into sections . . . and how sections translate into staff. And we have defined teaching supply and teaching demand. In the last example, we tried to reconcile the two—and alluded to the problem when the two are not in line. How to handle that problem will be dealt with below. But first—

Procedures to Follow

Now we need to get very practical. I'm going to give you the steps to complete this process culminating in a Staffing Worksheet that can be adapted for your school. As noted above, the master tally should be ready by mid-March. As soon as it arrives, the document is given to whoever is delegated with preparing the aforementioned staffing worksheets. Here are four helpful hints to jumpstart and organize the process:

√ Helpful Hint 12

On what we called Tally Day, meetings are scheduled at forty-five–minute intervals. These time slots can be adjusted (longer or shorter) depending on the size of your school. Generally, the principal, the administrator in charge of scheduling, and the respective department head are at each meeting, though there is no hard and fast rule as to who is invited. For example, you may want to include someone from guidance . . . an administrative intern . . . or, a representative from the scheduling committee.

English, the largest department, was traditionally scheduled first at 8:00 a.m. Fine Arts, the smallest department, came second at 8:45 a.m. (in case English ran overtime). Foreign Language, a medium-size department, was scheduled for 9:30 a.m. And then it was back to a large department, Social Studies, for 10:15 a.m. The process continued for the rest of the day, 11:00 a.m., 11:45 a.m., and so on, alternating big and small departments, for practical purposes. (Of course, we built in a lunch break.)

Here's another for keeping the faculty and staff informed:

√ Helpful Hint 13

It should be made abundantly clear to the faculty that this process is under way. Tally Day is advertised in advance. This is in keeping with my belief that scheduling should be done in a goldfish bowl. Such information should not be withheld from the staff. On the other hand, there is no question that a great deal rests on the decisions that will be made behind closed doors in terms of sections, staffing, and, yes, jobs. You might argue, then, that the process should not be advertised. It's like walking a tightrope. If one person knows what's going on, the whole school will know. It's better to be up front about the process taking place. At the same time, there needs to be a strictly enforced rule that the decisions made at these individual sessions are not to be shared with staff under any circumstances. If there is a leak, it will be easy to trace. To begin with, decisions made are first-round only, and conclusions drawn are premature. "Oh, my job has been cut," bemoans a first-year teacher. Not necessarily; this is a work in progress. Second, if one department head shares this information with teachers and others don't, there is a morale problem. Third, this information must go to central office, and ultimately board of education first. They should not learn this information from a teacher they run into in the frozen food aisle. All these guidelines must be observed, particularly confidentiality.

And another for developing a staffing worksheet to keep track of the numbers:

√ Helpful Hint 14

To make the process more uniform, I strongly recommend that you use a staffing worksheet similar to the one in this chapter. As noted above, once the master tally is in, someone is delegated with transferring that information to these sheets, one for every department.

Finally, one to keep totally organized for the process about to begin:

√ Helpful Hint 15

At this point, invest in a 1-1/2 inch loose-leaf binder with an index tab for each department. Also, start to color code each of the sheets. For example, in my school, the staffing worksheets were gold in color. When the papers start to fly—and fly they will—everyone can easily find the staffing worksheets, also known as "the gold sheets." By the end of Tally Day, you will have one gold sheet in each of the department sections.

Decision Making: Tally Meetings

Let's look at the staffing worksheet on the next page that has been filled in for the Fine Arts Department—and eavesdrop on the discussion among the principal, assistant principal, and department chairperson as they look at the numbers and decide how many sections of each course to offer. The only other given is that Art classes are capped (maximum) at twenty-five students because of the number of stations in art rooms. Ideally, however, the classes are smaller in size; the number "25" is the absolute limit. (You'll gradually master the "specs" for every course in your school.) Refer to the final two columns and the bottom row as decisions are made.

This past year the department ran twenty-three sections, translating into an FTE of 4.8 staff members. Put in terms of teacher time, Ms. Cezanne, Mr. Degas, Mrs. Picasso, and Dr. Renoir each taught five classes (five fifths); Ms. Van Gogh, the least senior member, was a part-timer who was the .8 (and taught four fifths). The total enrollment for Fine Arts classes was 504. Also keep in mind that these aren't necessarily 504 different students; some may have signed up for two (or more) art classes. However, as you make interyear comparisons, it is a good barometer of the draw of the department.

Let's start at the top of the list with Advertising and Design. For the current year, we are running three sections with a total of fifty-three students. The number eighty-two justifies adding a fourth section; you won't be able to get away with just three.

Crafts 1, which had one section last year with nineteen students, has almost doubled its enrollment. We'll run two next year. We have to be careful, though: Two courses and we've already added two additional sections.

Crafts 2, which also had one section last year, has drawn poorly. With a tally of only five we can't justify spending a precious section. Therefore, cancel this class and notify the counselors immediately so they can contact their students about picking an alternate,

USA High School Staffing Worksheet

Department _____ Chairperson _____

Code	Course	Current	Sections	Tallly	Projected	Comment
F101	Advertising & Design	53	3	82	4	
F102	Crafts 1	19	1	35	2	
F103	Crafts 2	18	1	5	x	Cancel
F104	Drawing & Painting	95	4	94	4	
F105	Photography (Fall)	17	1/	11	1/	Balance
F106	Photography (Spring)	19	/1	30	/1	Balance
F107	Studio in Art	226	10	201	9	Cut one
F108	Advanced Placement	11	1	22	1	
F109	Independent Study	13	1	TBD	1	
F109	Fashion Design	26	1	26	1	
F110	Computer Graphics	20	1	7	x	Cancel
Totals		**504**	**24**	**513**	**23**	

Current Sections	Staff Current	Sections Projected	Staff Projected	Net Change
24	4.8	23	4.6	−0.2

Note: 1. I use a slash mark to denote a half-year course. For example, one section of Photography is offered in the fall and one in the spring. Be very careful with those half-year courses. They count as only half a section. In terms of FTE, they are a tenth (0.1). Some schools use the same code for a half-year course offered both fall and spring and make the differentiation in the section number. In addition, some do not even specify "fall" or "spring" for a course such as this, but let the computer determine where it fits the best in the schedule.

if students haven't already done so. Or, with the approval of the department chair, giving some students the option of going into the Crafts 1 classes, so you will have a combined Crafts 1 & 2.[1] There is still a third option, which we will get to in a moment.

The decision for Drawing and Painting is a no-brainer. There are four sections for ninety-five students this year—and the tally for next year, ninety-four, is almost the same, so there will be four sections again next year.

Photography is a half-year (semester-long) course, so be careful with this one when counting sections. This year you have seventeen students in the fall and nineteen students in the spring. Each section counts as a tenth (two tenths = one fifth). In terms of teacher time, obviously this is .2 of a teacher's load. Think of the two semester-long courses as equaling one full-year course, again a .2. For next year, the total number is up slightly (41), but certainly not enough to justify an additional section. The problem is that the numbers are imbalanced between fall and spring. Guidance has to be instructed to shift students from spring to fall. Some schools do not specify "fall" and "spring" with regard to half-year courses. If the course is available both semesters (which isn't always the case), then they let the computer place that course where it fits in best.

Studio in Art is the foundations course, as you can tell by the 226 students enrolled in ten sections. At first, the chairperson projected running ten again for those 201 students. However, the numbers just don't warrant keeping ten sections—especially since we have already added two sections (Advertising & Design and Crafts 1). We can accommodate this tally with nine sections. We're going to project a cut of one section for the coming year.

Advanced Placement (AP) is tricky. This year, we're running one section for eleven students. The enrollment doubled for next year. However, we are not going to double the number of sections. That "11" was a borderline figure, with the class on the verge of cancellation, and we ran it even though the number was so low. The "22" for next year may be double, but it's just on the high side for one section. We'll keep it at one.

Independent Study is automatic. It's the only course for which the tally doesn't matter. View it as a one-room school house. The department gave up on advanced levels (level 3) for Advertising and Design, Drawing and Painting, Crafts, and others. Each year, they attracted only a handful of students, mostly art majors, never enough to warrant separate sections. Rather than canceling them, independent study/open studio was created whereby one teacher works individually with these highly motivated students.

Two new electives were added for the current year; how did they fare? Computer Graphics is currently debuting with one section of twenty students. For whatever reason, the course drew poorly for next year. Nine is a nasty number, yet you hate to cancel the class, and it doesn't lend itself to the independent study concept. The chairperson is asked whether she can recruit students over the next two weeks, to bring it up to . . . say, fifteen. She acknowledges some problems with the class itself. Although she appreciates the opportunity, she prefers to shelve the elective for a year, make some revisions, and then bring it back the following year. For starters, this course may need to be half-year, rather than full-year. Second, there was a constant problem trying to find a computer lab that was available when this class met. It turned out that, schoolwide, too many courses needed one of those labs at the same time. Third, there is concern as to whether the teacher assigned to this class was the best choice. Bottom line: Notify the guidance counselor that the class is canceled for the coming year.

---

[1] I'm using Arabic numerals (1, 2, 3, etc.). Some schedulers prefer Roman numerals (I, II, III, etc.). Either way is fine; just be consistent. Some colleagues steer clear of Roman numerals because of confusion between i, 1, I, and 1.

After all these tough calls, we end with an easy one. The other new elective, Fashion Design, drew twenty-six students this year and has the identical tally for next year. Hence, one section again.

You're done, at least for now, with the first draft of the tally worksheet. Add 'em up. With the additions and subtractions, you have 23 sections and a teaching need of 4.6. Most important, you show a net change in the teaching demand of –.2. Ms. Van Gogh, the part-timer, had an FTE of .8 or four fifths. As of now, she will have to be reduced by that .2 to .6. But remember: This is a first run-through. Numbers are sensitive and could change, even going the other way and justifying an additional section.[2] On the other hand, the numbers could further decrease, requiring a further cut. Decisions are not firm at this point, but at least you now have a starting point.

One more note of interest. Take a look at this year's total student registration (504) versus next year's (513). It's slightly higher—and yet you're down one section. How come? Remember what we said before about how sections break? Things worked a bit better for the scheduler this year. In other words, you were able to absorb a slightly larger number of students with one fewer section.

√ Helpful Hint 16

I called these the "green sheets." (Make them whatever color you want, just remember the advantage of using colored paper.) This will become the second page in the Fine Arts section of your scheduling notebook, right after the gold tally sheet. On this page, the chairperson will take the twenty-three agreed-upon sections and carve out a course load for each of the five teachers (actually, 4.6) in the department. Here is the green/load sheet filled in for Fine Arts following the staffing exercise we just did:

Teacher Course Loads for School Year

Department: <u>Fine Arts</u>   Chairperson: _____

Teacher	1st course	2nd course	3rd course	4th course	5th course
1. A. Cezanne	Drawing & Painting	Drawing & Painting	Studio	Studio	Photography Fall/Spring
2. B. Degas	Drawing & Painting	Drawing & Painting	Crafts	Crafts	Independent Study
3. C. Picasso	Advanced Placement	Studio	Studio	Studio	Fashion Design
4. D. Renoir	Advanced Design	Advanced Design	Advanced Design	Studio	Studio
5. E. Van Gogh	Advanced Design	Studio	Studio	X	X

---

[2]For some schools, this is it: The numbers will more or less hold and Step 4 is completed. At the other extreme, and the one used in this example, this is only a first run-through; the tallies will have to be revisited, perhaps more than once.

The department chairperson has one other task before leaving the office. She takes a blank copy of the Teacher Course Load Sheet for the next school year.

In the example above, Ms. Picasso may be assigned Advanced Placement, Fashion Design, and three sections of Studio in Art; Mr. Renoir may get three sections of Advertising & Design and two sections of Studio in Art. And so it goes . . . until all twenty-three sections have been assigned. The chairperson is given time, at least a week, to make these decisions and return the green sheet. She will want to consult with her teachers to get their input as well.

√ Helpful Hint 17

Where does the department head get the input for developing a course load for each teacher? Create a form, similar to the one below, for requesting *teacher preferences*. Generally, this step is done at a department meeting in January or February. In smaller schools, the task could fall to the master schedule builder. Either way, the process is the same. The teachers jokingly call this form the "dream" sheet; they just don't want it to turn into a nightmare.

Dear Department Member,

In the coming weeks, I will be working on your program for next year. Obviously, I can't satisfy *all* the requests, but I would like as much input as possible as I develop a course load for you. On the lines below, please indicate your program preferences for next year. Please give me several requests in rank order for each category. Return this form to me by the beginning of next week. Thank you.

_____

Department Head's Signature

1. I would like to teach the following subjects:
2. I would like to teach the following grade levels:
3. I would like to teach the following ability levels:
4. Other scheduling considerations:

_____

Teacher's signature/date

The process for Fine Arts is repeated for all the other departments. By the time Tally Day is over, you have determined your total *teaching demand* for the next school year. Put another way, you know the total number of sections needed to run the instructional program based on student course requests. Department heads have also been given their marching orders for developing course loads for each of their members. Note: We haven't said anything about reconciling it with the *teaching supply*. That comes next.

At this point in my scheduling workshop, the students do a major exercise in which they are given a school with 45 FTE (225 sections) and the master tally. It's their job to spend those 225 sections *very* wisely. I underscore that there are no right or wrong answers. Rather, they must be able to defend their decisions. It would be great if they could run every course; but unfortunately, sections are precious and they are forced to make some cuts. By design, they are going to have to make some very difficult decisions among competing choices, all drawn from my own scheduling career. This makes for an excellent lesson in Economics. Here are some of the toughest calls.

Let me reiterate that there are no single correct answers. I will tell you what *I* did; feel free to disagree based on your set of circumstances. I will provide the rationale for my thinking, but every school system is different. The classic example I start with: Do you run a Calculus class with a tally of only twelve? Some districts wouldn't think twice about keeping such a high-powered course, no matter what the enrollment; others have a minimum (usually 15–20) required before they will let the class run. Learn the ground rules in your own school/district. Remember: This is a partial list, the toughest calls in terms of number of sections to run. Hope for some no-brainers, like "English 11 Honors—47." It's safe to say that everyone would agree that two sections are needed. Others require quite a bit of thought. Those are the ones included below.

To simplify matters somewhat, we will operate with just two class sizes: thirty for academic classes and twenty for what we will call "Prep" or slower track classes. The first question I inevitably get is whether it is permissible to exceed those limits by one or two. I can't answer that question. In some districts, the class size maximum is strictly enforced, and with the thirty-first student, a new section must be formed. Other districts use the maximum as a guideline and make "every effort" to observe it, although the rule is not hard and fast. Ready? How many sections would *you* run?

Course	First Tally	Number of Sections	Comments
English 10 Honors	63	_____	
Social Studies 11 Honors	14	_____	
Social Studies 11 Advanced Placement	15	_____	double-period class
Economics (Honors)	10	_____	
Math 1X (Algebra— marginal)	60	_____	double-period class
Physics Prep (nonacademic)	7	_____	
Physics (academic)	56	_____	
Meteorology	8	_____	
Environmental Studies	7	_____	
Forensic Science	5	_____	
Oceanography	4	_____	
Genetics	9	_____	
Astronomy	3	_____	
Spanish 1	150	_____	
Spanish 4	11	_____	
Spanish 5	7	_____	

Course	First Tally	Number of Sections	Comments
Business Analysis 1	8	_____	
Business Analysis 2	7	_____	
Crafts 1	37	_____	
Crafts 2	14	_____	
Crafts 3	6	_____	

If you can handle these decisions, you will be able to deal with just about any in the future. As I said, I am going to give you *my* answers, although they are not necessarily the right answers. I will present my reasoning, and you can agree or disagree.

English 10 H (63): This is a coin toss that depends on whether you are permitted to slightly exceed the class size limit of thirty. I can see two sections, both slightly over thirty, or three sections of about twenty-one each. Suppose you go with the three; if you are desperate to find a section later on, you can always return and cut back to two.

Social Studies 11 Honors (14) and *Social Studies AP (15)—double period:* This is a very tough one. If you run both courses as they stand, you will be spending three sections (.6 in FTE) on a total of twenty-nine students. Did you forget to count the AP class as a .4 rather than a .2 since it is a double period? That's expensive and, frankly, I don't believe it's justified given the scarcity of sections. Even if the department agrees to run the AP course for one period instead of two (which is doubtful), you are still running two classes at fifteen or below. You have too many choices. I view the AP class as the honors alternative. Students who signed up for honors might be given a choice of going into the double-period AP course or reverting to the regular academic course.

Economics Honors (10): You need to get the numbers up, say to the threshold of fifteen. Give the department head a week to work with Guidance to recruit five additional students. If at the deadline he comes up empty or he feels that the new recruits are really not up to snuff and would water the honors class down, bite the bullet and drop Economics Honors, at least for the coming year.

Math 1X (60): The knee-jerk response is to say "two." However, keep in mind that these are the marginal students who are going to tackle a rigorous course that is challenging even for academic students. Also keep in mind that this course is already expensive because it is a double period. Nevertheless, it is pedagogically wise to run three sections of twenty rather than two sections of thirty. If you go with three sections, you're actually expending *six* sections. Costly, but I think it is necessary in this case.

Physics P (7) and *Physics (56):* In this example, you will start to see some of the creative solutions you can come up with. At first look, it would appear that the nonacademic version of Physics with only seven students should just be abolished. But, Science is a core course and odds are some juniors and seniors may be counting on this course in order to complete graduation requirements and/or science sequence requirements. So, consider running Physics "Prep." Here's another solution that can accomplish two objectives. Veteran schedulers will tell you that the academic version of Physics is typically one of the most difficult courses to load. In the real world, it frequently does have a lab period. Try finding two consecutive periods on a junior's schedule—or, even worse, a senior's schedule. With all the specialized courses, electives, and singletons they are taking, that's tough. If we were to run the Physics Prep, we would run two sections of Physics. To illustrate, we might schedule one on period 1 with a period 2 lab . . . and the other on period 7 with a period 8 lab. Hence, you have two shots to get a student loaded into the academic Physics class: periods 1 + 2 and 7 + 8. We are talking about upperclassmen who are completing their high school careers, so consider this solution: Group the seven "P" students with the fifty-six academic students. The total is sixty-three, which justifies *three* sections. So, you still have the 1 + 2 and 7 + 8, but now you can add a period 4 class with a period 5 lab. In summary, 1 + 2, 4 + 5, 7 + 8. You now have increased by 50 percent the possibility that students will be able to fit this double-period course into their schedules. It would be advisable to make this move in concert with Guidance. The new course would be called simply Physics. The teacher would have to be notified of this arrangement so that he could grade the "P" students differently.[3] It's a win-win-win situation. First, the "P" students are accommodated, despite the low tally; second, there are three sections of Physics instead of only two, much better for loading purposes; third, the three sections are all smaller in size.

Meteorology (8), Environmental Studies (7), Forensic Science (5), Oceanography (4), Genetics (9), Astronomy (3): In Step 1, we talked about feasibility. It is just not practical to offer so many different electives; look at the splintering effect. Something happened that severely diminished the enrollment for next year. Competing electives, teacher reputation, bad rap on the courses, or unfulfilled expectations are all possible explanations. In any event, we must deal with this messy situation. I'll offer four possibilities; there may be more. First, take all six and combine them into a new course called "Topics in Science" and devote about six or seven weeks to each. Second, turn them all into half-year courses. Third, pair them (Meteorology + Astronomy, Forensics + Genetics, or any other combinations you think would work). Fourth, develop a three-year rotation: Meteorology and Forensic Science will be offered next year . . . Environmental Studies and Astronomy the following year . . . Oceanography and Genetics the year after that . . . and then the rotation starts all over again the *fourth* year. The pairing and scheduling would depend on teacher availability. Also, it is imperative that a rotation such as this be widely publicized and prominently displayed in the course catalogue. You don't want any students to be disappointed when they learn (when it is too late) that a certain course will be offered only once in a three-year time span.

Spanish 1 (150): The obvious answer is five, which is certainly acceptable, but as you will see, these decisions are not always cookie cutter. Once again we have to let some pedagogy affect our decisions. The first year of a foreign language is critical in setting the foundations. If possible, run a sixth section and cut the average class size to twenty-five. This is a place you might choose to spend one of your sections in the name of education. It's also the first cut you might make if you can't come in within budget.

Spanish 4 (11) and Spanish 5 (7): Most workshop participants combine these two upper-level courses into one section, and that's also what many districts would

---

[3]Some schools might elect to run the two courses concurrently. In other words, there would be two course codes for the class: the "P" and the regular academic students. Other schools might be satisfied to just put them together. Another "your call." The purpose here is to show you all the possibilities.

probably do. But I recall an actual situation in which a parent petitioned the board, arguing that these two courses are not electives, but rather *sequential* courses. Her argument was that her son had already completed Spanish 4 and was entitled to 100 percent new instruction in Spanish 5, rather than a shared or combined class. She reiterated her point that a sequential course (1, 2, 3, etc.) is different from a purely elective class, which might be subject to combining. The board bought her argument and an additional .2 was allotted for the separate Spanish 5 section. Since then, I've been apprised of another creative solution to this type of problem. Because the fourth and fifth years in a foreign language are usually literature and culture classes (as opposed to grammar and language) with considerable latitude as to content, one district developed an alternate year curriculum for both—so that if the sections were combined, there would be different reading and other material from year to year so as to avoid repetition. Once again, my purpose here is to show you some of the creative solutions out there, not to campaign for any one in particular.

Business Analysis 1 (8) and Business Analysis 2 (7): Unlike Spanish 4 and 5, there is no reason why you can't combine these two into a single section to save both of them. There is little justification for running separate classes for a total of fifteen students.

Crafts 1 (37), Crafts 2 (14), and Crafts 3 (6): This is a fairly easy call by now. Run two sections of Crafts 1 and combine the Crafts 2 and 3 into a single section, either preserving both course codes in that class, or simply calling it Advanced Crafts.

The deliberations are over, the decisions have been made. You now have a total number of sections needed to run the program based on the tallies, that is, *teacher demand.* The superintendent has indicated the *teacher supply.* Hopefully the two are in line. If the principal is short, he may have to go back to the drawing board to make some more cuts, revisiting borderline decisions to reconcile supply and demand.

√ Helpful Hint 18

On Tally Day, keep a running list of the decisions you make so that the Guidance staff and department heads can be notified of what needs to be done in the days that follow. For example, "courses to be canceled," "courses for which to recruit," "courses to be combined," "courses on the cusp," and so on. One of my earliest mistakes was forgetting to notify counselors about canceled courses, which remained on student schedules until they emerged as "invalid codes" at the end of the line.

What happens if the demand and supply are miles apart? Of course, the scheduler can always beg, coax, and wheedle the superintendent into increasing teacher supply. Odds are that most requests will fall on deaf ears. Just maybe they can squeeze a section or two out of central office, but even that may be a long shot.

How to Bridge the Gap

Here is a comprehensive list of the methods for paring down the teacher demand if there is no wiggle room in the teacher supply. Even though I don't subscribe to all of them, I'm presenting a complete list of every technique I've seen tried:

1. Board Policy

With certain decisions, you have no choice. They have been made for you, usually by the Board of Education. For example, you may have a group of electives with tallies ranging from 8 to 14. Policy dictates that no class may run if it has fewer than fifteen students. Case closed. Become familiar with those givens in advance.

2. Low Enrollment Courses

Even without board policy, it makes sense to cancel classes with very low tallies. Unless your district is extremely well endowed, single-digit numbers is a good place to start. We're not talking about Special Education classes, which have a different set of guidelines. You may also find that Advanced Placement and other specialized classes manage to stay off the chopping block.

3. Mixing Levels

Sometimes it pays to put two levels of a course together if it means salvaging one or both. It worked when we combined Business Analysis 1 and 2 and again when we combined Crafts 2 and 3. It is easier to combine electives than sequential courses, but look what happened when we put Spanish 4 and 5 together.

4. Creative Combinations

In several cases, we put related electives together. For example, the splintering in the Science Department led to the potential pairing of six different electives, such as Meteorology and Astronomy.

5. Shifting Overages

Suppose three competing senior English electives broke badly. If money were no object, you'd add an additional section to each, but sections are precious so you have to be stingy. Add just a single section by moving students from two of the courses with overages to the third. It should be possible to find students who will agree to this move. I've been impressed by students' willingness to cooperate. Many don't have their hearts set on one particular elective, but if necessary, moves can be made on a lottery basis.

6. Recruiting

The example is readily apparent in Economics Honors. The chairperson was given a week to come up with additional students to bring the class up to the minimum required. Should he fail to find students or should the ones recruited be so weak so as to water down the honors section, it's better to cancel for next year.

7. Oversizing

As with board of education policy, this is likely to be a given; you probably have no choice. Does the teacher contract specify "every effort" to keep sections at a certain maximum, with a few exceptions permissible? Or, is it clearly stated that there is to be no oversizing whatsoever? Know this information before you start this process.

8. Limiting Enrollment

Limit enrollment for certain electives, usually based on class rank: seniors, then juniors, then sophomores, and so on. A popular course such as Auto Workshop is typical of those frequently oversubscribed. Not only does this save sections, but it also shifts underclassmen to their alternate choices, which frequently are smaller classes able to absorb additional students. Furthermore, those courses may depend on the alternates to make the cut. In addition, a school may have the staff, but not the facilities to accommodate all students who sign up for a course. Students may have to wait until they are older for a popular TV Studio elective because there isn't room for everyone.

9. Wait-Listing

Along these lines, wait-listing is another way to save sections. Don't necessarily jump to add an additional section for those highly specialized electives. (We're not talking about sequential required courses here). For such electives, form a waiting list (again, usually based on seniority) and encourage students to take other, less subscribed courses, ones you may be trying to fill for them to survive.

10. Alternate Year Offerings

Several examples were given: Rotating certain foreign languages on a three-year plan was one; rotating science electives over three years was a second. Here's a third: AP Chemistry never seemed to get off the ground; enrollment hovered around ten, barely breaking single digits. Year after year, the best students were left disappointed. Then it was realized that they could take this course as juniors *or* seniors. It was decided to offer AP Chemistry *every other* year. The students could plan their programs accordingly. In effect, the signups had doubled (two-year total) and this high-powered course was back on the scheduling board.

11. Multisection Courses

It's time to revisit decisions you made for courses with two or more sections. Maybe you can get by with seven instead of eight . . . or three instead of four. Remember the decision we made with regard to Spanish 1? With a tally of 150, we said that it was pedagogically wise to run six sections averaging twenty-five rather than five sections averaging thirty. Alas, when push comes to shove and there is no other alternative, you may have to revert to the larger class size to save a section.

12. "Frill Electives"

Note the quotation marks; it's really an oxymoron. I don't believe that any elective is a "frill," but in the real world (and when you have to make tough decisions), electives are often the first to go. I recall a heated discussion in which it was decided that "Guitar" would be cut. The rationale was that students could take private lessons without taking into account that some students couldn't afford them. The overriding argument was that required courses take precedence over electives.

13. Independent Study

Offering independent study is a very effective technique for saving sections while maintaining educational opportunities. There are two approaches. One is to provide it for a student who needs a course not otherwise offered, such as a post-Calculus course for an advanced Math student. What we did in Fine Arts with the advanced levels of Drawing and Painting, Advertising and Design, and so on, is a second. An open studio (aka Independent Study) is that one-room schoolhouse in which these art majors can take levels 3 and 4 of these courses that otherwise would have been canceled because none of the separate tallies was even close to sustaining a separate section. You will have to spend some teaching time for independent study. In Fine Arts, it was a .2, certainly a worthwhile investment. While this arrangement doesn't work for all subjects, it is a valuable weapon in your scheduling arsenal.

14. Extracurricular Activities

Certain curricular offerings might best be delivered as extracurricular activities. Suppose electives in Environmental Studies and School Law never seemed to get off the ground. Year after year they're canceled because of low enrollment, even though the administration didn't want to disappoint these students. The compromise solution was to create an ecology club and a student law court. Both proved to be popular with students and satisfied the demand for offerings in these areas at a far cheaper price than curricular offerings.

15. Distance Learning

Relatively new to the list is the concept of cooperative arrangements between neighboring schools. Suppose neither has the enrollment to sustain certain AP courses. School A runs one . . . and School B runs the other. Students in *both* schools are eligible for *both.* This sharing can be accomplished two ways: First, if the buildings are close enough, then busing can be arranged to transport students between the two. For this plan to work, the two schools have to follow the same bell schedules. Generally, the shared or co-op class is scheduled at the very beginning or end of the day. Second, the new "tech" version of such sharing is distance learning via cable television. Suppose neither school can sustain a course in Japanese or Latin. Each school offers one and students in the other can sit in on the class via cable hookup. Of course, it's not the same as actually sitting in the classroom, but teacher-student interaction is still possible with today's sophisticated equipment.

16. College Credit

This technique presupposes that the high school can make arrangements at a local college for advanced students to take courses it can't offer. Once again, there are two routes: One is to incorporate the course into the students' schedules if the college is close by and the schedules dovetail. The other option is for students to take the course on their own time: after school, evenings, or weekends. Many colleges are eager for such arrangements. It's to their advantage, drawing top students who enhance the college's reputation and just might end up on their campuses in the future. And, of course, there is a monetary consideration: Some tuition, albeit reduced, has to be paid—either by the district or by the student.

17. Online Instruction

This is still a work in progress, but it's the next generation of computer assisted instruction. This was a boon for students on the road: a semipro golfer on the circuit and a budding actress out of school more than she was in.

18. Graduation and Sequence Requirements

Be careful with your cuts. I already alluded to cavalierly canceling classes only to find that no matter how small the tally, they *had* to run because seniors needed them to graduate. Work closely with Guidance so your solution to one problem doesn't simply create a new problem. In concert, you may be able to make cuts while coming up with less costly alternatives to take their place.

19. Student Teachers

Almost last, and certainly least in my book, is the practice of oversizing classes where a "student teacher" or "associate" has been assigned. A slightly better, but still unacceptable option is assigning a paraprofessional or teaching assistant. My task here is to enumerate all the practices. This is one I don't favor. Fortunately, many board policies and/or teacher contracts prohibit this practice.

20. Borderline Decisions

You've gone through the master tally and the aforementioned list of ways to cut, and you now take another look at the teacher demand and teacher supply. Closer, but not close enough. You're still miles apart. Go back to the beginning and repeat the process a second time (and third, and fourth, if necessary). Review the master tally section by section; use these techniques to make even tougher cuts. Continue until teacher demand matches teacher supply.

Fortune Teller

Another title under your purview is that of fortune teller. In this chapter, you had to make some tough decisions with certain guidelines. While in the vast majority of cases things work out the way you had hoped, it doesn't always happen that way.

√ Helpful Hint 19

Maybe you can't get a crystal ball, but you can do the next best thing: Use projections from prior years to aid you in your decisions and limit the number of mistakes you make.

Track the histories; compare the tally for each course from this past year . . . to the actual enrollment on the first day of classes. Some courses have a consistent history of losing (or gaining) students after this point. Studying these patterns is helpful in making difficult decisions as to the number of sections per course.

Take a look at the chart below:

	March	June	September	October	January
Biology Prep	42	44	45	50	56
Journalism	16	14	14	12	10
Social Studies 10H	27	29	31	32	35

In the first example, it is obvious that Biology Prep is a course that tends to grow. Generally, the course draws from the academic Biology class whose students, intimidated by this course, drop down to this level. Look at the numbers. There is a slow but steady growth through the spring that continues once the course starts up in the fall.

Journalism is a different case altogether. It is an elective, and in this school it is expected that a course have *at least* fifteen students preregistered before it is permitted to run. You're cutting it awfully close. As you can see, 16 is the *highest* number the course ever attracts. It is downhill from the beginning. For a variety of reasons (discussed later), the course dips well below the threshold of fifteen.

The final example, Social Studies 10 Honors, depends on the stability of the tenth grade AP European Studies. You *may* need to leave some growing room in case there is a history of students dropping down a level from that rigorous AP course.

Before we conclude Step 4, I want to return to a question alluded to earlier. When students didn't qualify for Honors or AP classes, I often heard the following proposition: "Let my son start out in the class. If he can't hack if after the first marking period, he can always drop down to the regular class." Now that we've completed Step 4, you can understand why this is impractical. In essence, it's double dipping—holding a tally in *two* places. This solution might work in an isolated case, but imagine what will happen if this practice occurs wholesale and students sign up for one course . . . with their eyes on an alternate "just in case" the first one doesn't work out. Unless money is no object and there is no limit on sections (highly doubtful), avoid this practice.

Summary

- The master tally is in, with preregistration figures for each and every course.
- Tallies become sections and sections become staff.
- The job of the scheduler is to reconcile *teacher demand* (the total number of sections needed) with *teacher supply* (the budgeted number of FTEs and corresponding sections). Procedures for Tally Day, developing a staffing worksheet, meeting with department heads, and making the critical decisions were reviewed.
- A list of twenty techniques for bridging the gap between demand and supply was enumerated. It was emphasized that this is not an exact science; the scheduler has to be a fortune teller to make all the right calls, and that comes with experience.
- While he may not have a crystal ball, he *does* have the past enrollment for each course to guide him in making some of those close calls.
- This step concluded with a warning not to encourage students to double dip— sign up for one course, thinking that a switch to another (usually a lower level) is automatic if the first one doesn't work out for them. You don't have the resources to permit this.

TASKS FOR STEP 4

You need an *effective* and *efficient* way to determine the number of sections for each course in every department, as well as the utilization of staff.

- Organize and carefully orchestrate plans for Tally Day.
- Design a *staff projection* worksheet.
- Design a teacher *dream sheet*.
- Design a *teacher course load worksheet*.
- Develop uniform procedures for deciding on the number of sections per course.
- Look on e-Bay or at garage sales for a crystal ball.

Step 4 is an especially *critical* step, one everyone needs to understand.

Step 5

Spot Trouble

The Conflict Matrix

Step 5 is the most technical step. For that reason, some schedulers tend to bypass it altogether. That's not a good idea. Extremely valuable information can be gained from this step, which is a precursor to building the master schedule itself.

The Problem

It's easier to "do" a conflict matrix than to explain it. Let me begin with a story that makes the point.

Poor Mary discovered at the end of her senior year that she had failed two subjects needed in order to graduate: Health and Economics. She dutifully reported to the registrar to sign up for those two courses in the three-period–day summer school that, if passed, would enable her to graduate in August. When she went to register, however, she was informed that she *still* wouldn't be able to graduate. Why?

> - Mary needs those two subjects to graduate.
> - Health is being offered *only* once—on period 2.
> - Economics is also being offered *only* once—and also on period 2.
> - Obviously, Mary can't be in two places at the same time.
> - Mary has what we call a *scheduling conflict.*

A *scheduling conflict* occurs when two (or more) subjects are offered at the same time, and the student must make a choice between the two. This is the simplest definition; we'll complicate it gradually as we move through the process.

But the question at hand: Could this conflict have been avoided? Perhaps—if the master scheduler had used a vital tool called the conflict matrix to *spot trouble*. Simply put, the conflict matrix enables you to pinpoint which courses are taken in tandem so that they can be placed on different periods. Simply put—but not so simply done. That is why some schedulers skip this step altogether and place sections without consulting the matrix. It's like throwing darts with a blindfold on.

Suppose you, and I, and two of our friends have all signed up to take French 3 and Business Analysis, both single section courses. At least four of us have those courses in common. *The scheduler should not place these sections on the same period when building the schedule.* If he does, at least four of us will be out of luck and required to make a forced choice between the two, perhaps unnecessarily. Without the matrix, however, he has no idea that there is a potential problem and one that can be avoided.

Put another way: Take a high school in which many seniors sign up for Advanced Placement (AP) courses in various combinations. You are working with an eight-period day, but you have to place nine AP courses. It's the old "nine-pound baloney in the eight-pound bag" trick. Or the old game of musical chairs. Something's got to give.

To illustrate, suppose you have to place a section of Advanced Placement Art. Take a look at the following list. It indicates the potential conflicts with AP Art. In other words, the number next to the course indicates the number of students who have signed up for *both* courses. If you place both courses at the same time (period), then all of these students are out of luck and will have to choose between the two:

AP Music	15
AP English	12
AP Psychology	11
AP Government	10
AP Biology	8
AP Spanish	6
AP French	4
AP Calculus	2

The obvious question: AP Art has to be placed at the same time (same period) with one of these. Which would you choose? There should be *no* question: AP Calculus. According to the chart—which came from the matrix—only two students are taking both courses in common. Only two students will be forced to make a choice. It's unfortunate that even two will be forced into this situation—but that's better than six, or eight, or ten. *Without the conflict matrix, you wouldn't have known this information.* Now, to make the point, imagine if you had arbitrarily placed AP Calculus and AP Music on the same period: A staggering fifteen students would have been out of luck. I hope you see how important it is to spot trouble in advance and to learn how to use the matrix.

Two footnotes to this illustration: Veteran schedulers may have picked up on the fact that we didn't necessarily have to pit Music against Calculus. In other words, it is possible that, say, Biology and French have no conflict between them. True. More about that below. I use this example because it successfully introduces the concept.

Second, I have come across schools that use the same master schedule year after year. They don't go through this process on an annual basis. In essence, the students have to make their requests fit the schedule, rather than the other way around. Not a good idea. Step 4 must be repeated. Yes, there can be many similarities, year in year out—but some things change. Take the example just given. For instance, next year there are few if any conflicts between Advanced Placement Art and Music . . . while the conflicts between Art and Calculus have tripled to six. This information will obviously affect the decisions you make as you start to place sections.

Definitions and Illustrations

Before proceeding, let me define three simple terms that will come up as we work through the next three steps:

- A *singleton* is a course that will meet only once in the schedule; in other words, it is a single section course.
- A *doubleton* is a course that meets twice in the schedule; there are *two* sections of this course.
- A *tripleton*, then, is a course that meets three times in the schedule; there are *three* sections of this course.

Take a look at the tallies and sections for USA High School's upcoming summer school. This is our first attempt at building a master schedule. Since it's small, it's a good place to start.

Subject	Tally	Section(s)	Periods Offered
English 11	25	1	_____
English 12	85	3	1–2–3
Economics	23	1	_____
Government	39	2	not when Economics meets
Math 12	87	3	1–2–3
French 3	27	1	_____
Spanish 3	26	1	_____
Biology	80	3	1–2–3
Chemistry	21	1	_____

As you will learn as we get closer to Step 6, building the master schedule involves using as much "given information" as possible because givens reduce the degree of choice. Picture, for example, a jigsaw puzzle. We usually start with the corner pieces because we know where they go. Furthermore, by taking them out of the pile, we have reduced the degree of choice (the size of the pile) in placing the other pieces. So it is with scheduling: Place the givens and reduce the degree of choice. In this case, the tallies indicate that three of the courses merit three sections. It's another one of those no-brainers. If there are three sections and three periods—place one section on each of the three periods: *1–2–3.* The course is now offered on all three of the summer school periods, and this will ensure that the maximum number of students can enroll in those three courses without a conflict. The placement of Economics and Government is not quite as simple, but there is a piece of given information here as well: Economics and Government will be taught by the same teacher (all three periods). While we don't know those period placements yet, we do know that the two sections of Government will *not* be when Economics meet. In other words, that singleton and doubleton will go together—periods 1–2–3. Once the conflict matrix has dictated when Economics is scheduled, Government will be assigned the remaining two periods.

In addition to Economics, there are four other singleton classes to be assigned: English 11, French 3, Spanish 3, and Chemistry. Just how do we pick periods for these classes? Let's turn to our first conflict matrix (below):

- Note that all of the five singleton classes are at the top of the columns and at the beginning of the rows.
- In the real world, course codes (rather than titles) are sometimes used. Obviously, titles are easier, but they are larger and don't always fit.
- The numbers are at the intersection points of two courses; for example, the "2" under Economics is where it intersects with English. This simply means that *two* students are taking both English and Economics, and if you schedule both courses at the same time, *two* students will be forced to make a choice.
- It doesn't matter where you start, row or column; the point of intersection produces the same number. Economics . . . English (2); English . . . Economics (2).
- A double dash is used in this particular model where a course intersects with itself. Obviously, no conflicts.

	English	Economics	French	Spanish	Chemistry
English	—	2	3	6	13
Economics	2	—	13	11	1
French	3	13	—	0	16
Spanish	6	11	0	—	2
Chemistry	13	1	16	2	—

Find the bad combinations. Answer these three questions to test your understanding:

1. What does the "11" on the Spanish row mean?

2. What is the worst conflict on the matrix?

3. What will happen if Spanish and French are scheduled at the same time?

First, the "11" means that there are eleven potential conflicts between Economics and Spanish. Second, the worst conflict on the matrix is the "16" between Chemistry and French; imagine what would happen if you *didn't* use the matrix and accidentally scheduled both singletons for the same time slot. Third, there is no conflict between French and Spanish; hence, as we shall see below, there is no problem (for now, anyway) with assigning both singletons to the same period. When we get to Step 6, we'll see other types of conflicts: "teacher" (one teacher teaching two singletons) and "room" (for special facilities such as computer labs).

We're ready to build our first master schedule using the conflict matrix. Again, there are other factors to consider that we will introduce as we move along, but we will get to them in time. For now, let's focus only on the conflict matrix.

Some of those aforementioned factors may determine where we start, but I'm going to start with English. And for the sake of argument, I'm going to place English 11 on period 1. To repeat: I might have started with another subject . . . another period . . . but for this first demonstration, I'm keeping things simple.

Let's go in order: Where shall we place Economics? If we put it on period 1, with English, how many students will have a conflict? We've already said—two. At this point, why should any students have a conflict? We won't use period 1 again (for now, anyway), and we'll assign Economics to period 2. So far so good.

Continuing, we come to French. Let's review the possibilities: If we place it on period 1 (same time as English), the matrix tells us that three students will be forced to make a choice. Not terrible . . . but perhaps these three can be saved. However, if we put French on period 2 (same time as Economics), a whopping thirteen students will be out of luck. That certainly should be avoided. We've used periods 1 and 2, but we haven't used period 3 yet. So period 3 it is for French. Obviously, no conflicts. But now we're out of periods and will have to use 1, 2, and 3 again.

Let's reverse the process. Take a look at the Spanish row (or column); what course will produce the *fewest* conflicts? According to the matrix, there are "0" conflicts between French and Spanish. French was already placed on period 3, so we'll place Spanish 3 at the same time: period 3. Why not?[1]

The final course to schedule is Chemistry—and once again, we'll make our decision based on the matrix. We can use period 1, 2, or 3. Which will yield the fewest conflicts for Chemistry? There is only one conflict between Economics and Chemistry. Economics has already been placed on period 2; we'll place Chemistry on period 2 as well.

All five classes have been successfully scheduled with a total of just one conflict! Of course, this example was oversimplified, but it makes the point. Imagine what would have happened if we had left these period placements to chance. There might have been scores of conflicts, given the numbers showing up on the matrix. To repeat: By using this invaluable tool, only one student will be put into a forced-choice situation. I hope that you are beginning to understand why schedulers must consult the conflict matrix as they start to place sections and build the master.

√ Helpful Hint 20

From this point on, get into the habit of using only red pen and regular pencil to indicate your scheduling decisions. Singleton classes, such as the five above, should be written in red ink. They are *unchangeable*. If you change even one, there could be a domino effect in terms of conflicts created. Use pencil for any other period placement that is *not* locked and that *is* subject to change. In the heat of scheduling a few steps down the road, you may forget. Therefore, red ink for what *cannot* be changed and erasable pencil for what *can* be changed. When we get to Step 6, the actual building of the schedule, there will be 101 reasons to tempt you to change your mind on a decision (based on the conflict matrix) already made. *Don't do it.*

---

[1]As I just mentioned, the "why not" is that other factors may impinge on your decisions. For example, you may find that the same Foreign Language teacher is hired to teach both French and Spanish—and she can't be at two places at the same time—even though there are different students. But, we'll get to those complicating factors later on. According to the matrix, French and Spanish can be at the same time, at least for now.

The conflict matrix has taken on added importance in recent years as the number of singletons has proliferated. Years ago, there were far many more multisection courses, obviously easy to place in building the master schedule. However, with more singletons (and doubletons and tripletons)—as opposed to those multisection courses—placement of sections must be done more thoughtfully *if* conflicts are to be *minimized*. Note that I didn't say *eliminated*. Given the number of singletons, some conflicts will remain, but the scheduler's goal is to keep them to an absolute minimum.

Of course, the number of conflicts will depend in large measure on your curriculum. A school with limited electives that has mostly multisection courses (10 sections of English 9, 8 sections of Social Studies 11, etc.) will have fewer conflicts, but far less academic choice. On the other hand, a school with numerous elective offerings will have far greater choice, but numerous *potential* conflicts. There are schools that have more than 120 singletons to be placed over an eight-period day. Do the math: There would be as many as fifteen singletons on each of the periods. Where each would be placed has to be given *very* careful forethought.

Why are there so many singletons? A story is worth a thousand words. Early in my scheduling career, one school experimented with its first elective in the Social Studies Department. Topical matter coupled with a dynamic teacher who created the course generated eight sections of that course at its high point. Certainly easy to schedule: one section on each of eight periods. But then things started to change. For one, more electives were added and suddenly this course, which heretofore had had a "monopoly," now had competition. Second, the graduation requirements in that district changed, and students had less room on their schedules for electives. Third, the size of the student body decreased slightly—and with it there was less demand for all electives. Fourth, there was a changing of the guard and with that turnover came new teachers teaching this elective; none, unfortunately, had the draw of the teacher who had designed the course. So for these four reasons, the number of sections for this elective ebbed, going from eight to seven to six, and ultimately down to just one. It, too, became a singleton. Unfortunately, this is frequently a fact of life in the scheduling world.

Why is a conflict-free schedule so very difficult? While there are some trends (students taking certain high-level courses in tandem), frequently there is no pattern as to which electives are taken together. Follow this scenario:

- Sally wants AP Art and AP Economics
- Harry wants AP Economics and French 5
- Irene wants French 5 and Chorus
- Tommy wants Chorus and Crafts 2
- Jane wants Crafts 2 and Advertising Design
- Murray wants Advertising Design and AP Art

Variety may be the spice of life, but it is also the bane of the master scheduler.

Conflict Matrix Formats

I have underscored the value of using the conflict matrix, yet many novice schedulers approach this step with trepidation and avoidance. Why? Simple: The conflict matrix can be unwieldy, obstreperous, and laborious—just to list a few unflattering adjectives. Let's take a look at five common formats in which the conflict matrix is generated to see if we can make the task less arduous.

1. Manually Produced

Earlier I noted that *two* documents are delivered on Tally Day. The computer generates the master tally and the conflict matrix at the same time. As a matter of fact, think of the conflict matrix as just a different form of the tally, showing the *combinations* of courses taken in tandem.

But what about a school that does not have a software package that produces a conflict matrix? Almost all such packages worth their salt have a conflict matrix component. If yours doesn't, maybe you should shop around for a better one. As I will explain below, there is tremendous competition among vendors for your business. If anything, the competition has produced more user-friendly matrices, shown later.

However, there are smaller schools that still do everything manually. Although the computer can produce the matrix far more easily, one can be done by hand. Suppose you're talking about a small school, alternative school, summer school, or school with a relatively small degree of choice. You can hand tally all the combinations. This involves going through all the course requests for each student. Again, this is possible only with a small student population and relatively few courses.

Look at this example. I have **bolded** the courses that Mary is taking. She has to select one course in each area (English, Math, Science, Language, Elective, Physical Education). There is no choice in Social Studies because all students take the basic ninth grade course; there is no ability grouping in that department.

Student Scheduling Card

English 9
English 9 Honors

Social Studies 9

Math IX
Math I
Math I Honors

Science 9
Science 9 Honors

French I
Spanish I
Italian I

Required Art
Required Music

Physical Education
Team Sports

Get some graph paper, a pot of coffee, and begin. Make sure that there are no interruptions. You can knock this off in a relatively short period of time if you work undisturbed. Ask another person to work with you: counselor, administrator, secretary, intern.

Mary is taking: English 9 Honors and Math 1, English 9 Honors and Science 9, English 9 Honors and Spanish 1, English 9 Honors and Required Music, English 9 Honors and Team Sports. That's five slash marks already. Note that I omitted Social Studies; all ninth graders take the same course so there is no need to include it in the matrix. For that matter, you may eliminate some of the other courses you know will be multisection. For example, in Physical Education, you may go into this knowing that there will be only one section of Team Sports while all the other sections will be regular Physical Education. You can probably omit Physical Education as you build this matrix by hand. Every omission will save precious time and effort.

But we're not done. Now let's look at the combinations with Math 1. We already took care of English and we're not involving Social Studies. So, we have Math 1 and Science 9, Math 1 and Spanish 1, Math 1 and Required Music, and Math 1 and Team Sports. Fewer and faster; tally them all.

Let's move on to Science 9: with Spanish 1, Required Music, and Team Sports. We're down to three. You get the idea.

There comes a point when there are too many students and/or too many courses to build the matrix this way. If your school doesn't plan to get a software package to do this job for you, you may have to rely on past experience and intuition. For example, you know that, logically, Math 1 Honors and Science 1 Honors tend to have the same students. I didn't say that there was a 100 percent correlation; there doesn't have to be. But as you build the master schedule, it makes sense to put these two courses on two different periods. Or, you know from past experience that the students who take Team Sports also tend to be the Music students. Then, separate those two periods. Some creative schedulers report using programs such as Excel and Access to design their own homemade conflict matrix. Bottom line: You can get by without the matrix.

2. Dot Matrix Format

The example used for summer school is in dot matrix format. It was easy to read because there were only five singleton courses. Now try using that format with a large high school with several hundred courses, say 300. You can wallpaper your office with the grid: 300 courses across and 300 down. In a very large high school there may be even more courses. Dealing with such a matrix is highly unwieldy. You have to circle the highest numbers, go through the grid to determine the intersection points, and then figure out what courses they represent, all very carefully. Besides graph paper and pots of coffee, include extra strength aspirin with your supplies. It is a laborious exercise, and probably the reason some schedule builders skip this step. Fortunately, the new generation of computer packages provides more efficient methods. Unfortunately, the dot matrix format still prevails in some systems.

3. Tally Restriction

Assuming your package uses the dot matrix format, you don't have to include every single course in the school. For example, let's say that Social Studies 10 has the highest tally with 10 sections. You know that there will be at least one section on every period. Omit it. Or, Spanish 2: You have determined that the tallies warrant five sections. Again, don't include it in the matrix. As a rule of thumb, I would definitely include singletons, doubletons, and possibly tripletons. Which of these courses would you exclude from the conflict matrix if you could limit the number?

Math 11	100
Spanish 3	125
Spanish 3 Honors	23
Journalism	19
Studio in Art	47

Just how do you tell the computer to scale down the number of courses it includes when building the conflict matrix? There are three routes to go; which you elect depends on your software package. Some permit you to exclude certain courses (which you know from experience are unnecessary) before the matrix is generated; some allow you to delete certain courses once the first draft of the matrix is produced; still others let you indicate the cut-off for including courses in the matrix. This last example is probably the most common, and if you have a choice, the best avenue to take. Suppose that thirty is the average class size in your school. Keep in mind that when the conflict matrix is generated, you haven't completed the tally worksheets yet; in other words, you haven't determined the number of sections for each course. So what do you tell the computer? Let it do the math: To restrict the number of courses in the matrix, set a threshold of, say, ninety students. In other words, include only those courses that have a sign-up of ninety or fewer. These are your potential tripletons. Even with a class size of thirty, the cut-off of ninety is not a hard-and-fast rule. Maybe you're more comfortable with as many as 100, or prefer to further reduce the size of the conflict matrix and want only courses with eighty or fewer. Bottom line: The conflict matrix that results will be far more manageable.

In the example above, I would include Spanish 3 Honors, Journalism, and Studio in Art; I would exclude Math 11 and Spanish 3, because given their tallies (both 100+), they won't be involved in any conflict decisions.

4. Course Restriction

One of the most useful tools I have discovered is a custom-made conflict matrix including only those courses I told the computer to include.

√ Helpful Hint 21

For example, I called for a matrix that included only Advanced Placement courses, and/or another that included only Honors classes, and/or a third that included both Advanced Placement and Honors classes, and/or a fourth that contained all the free-standing electives. You can come up with anything that works for you, assuming, of course, that your software package can do it.[2] These were extremely helpful resources when I started to actually build the schedule and place periods.

---

[2] I will restate that there is tremendous competition for your business. If you are not getting features that you want, don't be shy about contacting the vendor. Or, you may find that there is a users group for that company that can tell you what is and isn't possible. Collectively you may have more clout. The new editions of software packages are constantly upgraded. It makes for a great lesson on the value of competition.

5. Course Listing

The fifth and final model for the conflict matrix is the one in which the mule work has been done for you. It's similar to the example above for Advanced Placement Art. A list is printed for each course with its worst conflicts, usually in descending order. Here's another for English 12 Honors. The parameters were set so that only courses with fewer than thirty were included in the matrix. Look at the valuable information you net:

Advanced Placement Government	18
Spanish 5	10
Advanced Placement Physics	8
Environmental Studies	6
French 5	3
Advanced Placement Art	2
Crafts 2	1
Journalism	1

Interesting results. Advanced Placement Government is the heavy hitter. Put those two courses at the same time, and you know by now what will happen. As you start to assign periods in the next step, you will know to keep those two apart. Work your way down the list in numerical order, from the highest to the lowest number of conflicts. How far down you will be able to go will depend on the number of periods with which you have to work as well as other competing conflicts. Suffice it to say, you'll worry about the "ones" (Crafts 2 and Journalism) last. Of course it would be nice to avoid conflicts for these individuals, too, but you have to worry about the bigger numbers first. We never promised a conflict-free schedule—but rather a conflict-*reduced* schedule.

Beyond Singletons

It is not only the singletons that can cause conflicts. As you become more experienced, you will see how doubletons and tripletons can prove problematic:

Wood	2nd and 3rd periods	Two choices . . .
Ceramics	2nd and 3rd periods	One can go 2nd, one can go 3rd
Music Theory	2nd and 4th periods	Still have another period to use
Keyboarding	3rd and 4th periods	Four subjects, three periods = trouble!

Sometimes a combination of multisection courses meeting on the same periods can be just as troublesome. Follow this scenario; the periods used are **bolded:**

French 2	**6th**	
Math 2X	6th and **8th**	
Chorus	**4th** & 8th	
Ceramics	**1st** & 6th	
Social Studies 10	1st, 4th, 6th, & 8th	4 sections—but nothing is left!

> ### √ Helpful Hint 22
>
> So far we have been talking about singletons. But what about doubletons and tripletons? It would be great if we could give them the same attention, but we don't always have the time (or periods) to review each of those decisions. However, I have found the following trick very useful when assigning periods wholesale—which is about to begin in Step 6. With doubletons (and tripletons), I noticed that sometimes I was arbitrarily assigning periods, say 3 and 6, or 4 and 8, and the like (for doubletons), or 1, 2, and 5; and 3, 5, and 7, and so on (for tripletons). Just by sheer accident, I tended to use the same combination more than once. To prevent that from happening, I kept a running list of doubleton and tripleton combinations to avoid using the same combination of periods more than once, and thereby further reduced the possibility of a conflict. Of course, as we are about to see, certain period assignments are dictated by other variables we haven't yet discussed. Still, there is considerable latitude, given the facts that there are so many periods with which to work. For example, the doubleton chart looked something like this: 3 & 4; 2 & 5; 4 & 8; 6 & 7; 1 & 8; 1 & 5; 3 & 5

Summary

The purpose of the conflict matrix is simple: *Why guess?* It lets you spot trouble before it happens. Why should a student have a scheduling conflict, that is, a forced choice, unnecessarily? Eliminating conflicts is a tall order, but using the matrix the number can be drastically reduced.

Unfortunately, using the matrix is not quite as simple as understanding its purpose. For some schedulers, this has become a dreaded step. To begin with, they may not have access to a computer scheduling software package that produces a matrix. Or, the package may produce a matrix that is unwieldy. Current software packages are more sophisticated and have come a long way in making this laborious task far more manageable. Shop around, if you can. This is a critical step in the process and you have to master it, so you might as well get the best tools you can.

We saw how the use of the matrix can significantly reduce the number of conflicts. Without it, the scheduler is essentially playing Pin the Tail on the Donkey with period placement.

TASKS FOR STEP 5

Working with the conflict matrix is a highly technical skill and should be reserved for the scheduler herself or a member of the scheduling team who is extremely attentive to detail. However, there are decisions governing its use that will have to be made collectively. The liaison between the scheduler and the building and/or district computer expert will be particularly important. By the time this step is completed, the scheduler should have a list of courses that are taken in tandem so they can be placed on different periods. Not only singletons, but also doubletons and tripletons have to be considered.

The master schedule has begun to take shape. The skeleton is in place; in the next step you will flesh it out with the remaining sections.

Step 6

Build It

Construction of the Master Schedule

At last we're ready to *build* the master schedule itself. *First*, we'll take care of some housekeeping matters. *Second*, we'll review a long list of variables to be considered. *Third*, we'll examine a variety of methods, tricks of the trade, used by veteran schedulers. *Fourth*, we'll look at how these variables are juggled and interact. *Fifth*, we'll investigate the framework for laying out the periods. *Sixth*, we'll introduce the personnel factor into the equation. And *seventh*, I'll provide some simulated data so you can go through the exercise of building a master schedule on your own.

Setting Up Shop

The preliminaries are complete. You're ready to put red pen and pencil to paper, and start construction of the full master schedule for your school. However, there are several amenities that need to be taken care of first:

• You and your colleague(s) need to work uninterrupted. Yes, you have other responsibilities, especially during the second half of the year, but these need to be delegated so you can give 100 percent of your attention to this project. First, this is heavy detail work; interruptions can cause costly errors. Second, you need to devote all of your attention to the decisions to be made. Third, starting and stopping is inefficient. Barring some earth-shattering event, insist on quality time. I used to joke about renting a motel room—but realized that might not look good. Odds are you have to remain on campus, close to your office, and near the resources you need for making decisions. A good secretary can double as a security guard to make sure you are not interrupted.

> ### √ Helpful Hint 23
>
> Delegate an assistant principal to cover for you. Yes, you are still in the building, but you need to be sequestered. Pretend that you are attending a conference; your assistant would cover for you under those circumstances. Let her do so now.

- You need a dedicated work area. Don't plan on setting up each morning and packing up each night. Ideally you have a conference room or, at the very least, a conference table that can remain undisturbed for the entire process.

- You must ensure security and privacy. While I have preached running the scheduling process in a goldfish bowl, during the building phase this is a "work in progress" and not ready for public consumption.[1]

- Still, keep the staff informed. Remember: There are no secrets in a school. At a faculty meeting or at an early morning briefing, announce that the process is about to begin and that you need to be sequestered. Explain the need for a news blackout, since decisions are tentatively definite—and definitely tentative. Throughout this book, I have stressed the importance of being aboveboard with staff. This is yet another example.

- Many people love building the schedule, putting together a giant jigsaw puzzle. However, it can be frustrating, too. Make sure to step away occasionally and take several short breaks as well as time for lunch. You will work much more efficiently afterwards. Yes, it's addictive, but you'll benefit from some distance, too. Some administrators "schedule scheduling"—setting objectives for each day (e.g., complete one large and one small department).

- Stock up on supplies reflecting your working style. You must be methodical and orderly. Markers, red pens, pencils, folders, push pins, and so on. Wire baskets were my favorites; I wanted to know where to find resources (conflict matrix, master tally, etc.) as well as have a secure place for completed pages: staffing worksheets (gold), teaching assignments (green), and first draft of the schedule for each department (pink).

- Photocopy a healthy supply of scheduling grids based on the number of periods in your school and maximum number of teachers in any one department. Customize the number of rows and columns to fit your situation. Here is a sample.

Teachers/Periods	1	2	3	4	5	6	7	8
1								
2								
3								
4								

(Continued)

---

[1]During lunch, a snoopy colleague sneaked a peak and noticed that a colleague's name was off the schedule. Within hours, rumors spread that she didn't have a job for next year. The fact is, that just before the break, we were deciding whether to use her married or maiden name.

(Continued)

Teachers/Periods	1	2	3	4	5	6	7	8
5								
6								
7								

> **√ Helpful Hint 24**
>
> Photocopy these 8-1/2 × 11 grid sheets in three colors: pink (1st draft), yellow (2nd draft), blue (final working copy). Remember what I said above about the importance of color coding. Once the papers start flying—and fly they will—it will be a great deal easier to find things if they are in color. Try to find something on a cluttered desk with just white paper; it can be difficult, if not impossible. Color coding is at the top of my hint list.

- Finally, pamper yourself with a few creature comforts: a pot of good coffee . . . homemade cookies or donuts . . . perhaps some good classical music in the background. Let's face it: You're in for the long haul; make it as warm and fuzzy as possible.

Thirty Factors to Consider When Building the Master Schedule

Without a doubt, this section is the most important in the book. Read it carefully. Perhaps not all of these variables apply to your school, but most will. These are key issues to be discussed with your administrative colleagues and/or scheduling committee.

1. Conflict Matrix Decisions

You've already completed Step 5. By now you have assigned periods to the singleton (and hopefully doubleton, and maybe even tripleton) classes. *These are untouchable.* Write them in red and do not change them. Even one small shift can cause a domino effect. Record these decisions in two places: on the grid for the department and on a separate minimaster for singletons. Keep one for each of the special populations: Advanced Placement (AP) classes . . . honors classes . . . remedial classes . . . singleton electives . . . and any others unique to your school.

As explained in Step 5, the conflict matrix decisions form the skeleton of the master schedule around which other sections will be placed. One more time: You may be tempted later to change them to solve other problems; *don't even think about it.*

2. Block Schedules

These are alternative schools or school-within-school programs in which students move as a block: programs for at-risk youth, Special Education self-contained

---

√ Helpful Hint 25

Here's what a minimatrix would look like for Honors and Advanced Placement classes. Remember: This information is entered by hand as the sections are placed. You can see just by inspection how few conflicts there are.

Period/Grade	1	2	3	4	5	6	7	8
9th	English 9H	Math 9H	Social Studies 9H	English 9H		Science 9H	Spanish 9H	Social Studies 9H
10th	Spanish 10H	English 10H	AP European History		Math 10H	Math 10H	Science 10H	Social Studies 10H
11th	AP American History	English 11H	Social Studies 11H	AP Biology	Spanish 11H	Math 11H	English 11H	Chemistry H
12th	AB Calculus	English 12H	Math 12H	AP Chemistry	AP English; Social Studies 12H	AP Physics	AP Spanish	AP Government/ Economics

---

programs, honors academies, small learning communities, English as a Second Language classes. If you have such programs, superimpose them on the master schedule *before* you start so you know what periods and/or facilities are off the table.

3. Number of Periods

The number of periods runs the gamut:

- Schools with block scheduling may have as few as four block (double) periods during the course of the day.
- Conversely, a large urban high school may require as many as fourteen periods.
- Some suburban schools, bursting at the seams, are adding on a period or two to the regular eight- or nine-period day.
- Even suburban schools *not* bursting at the seams are adding periods to accommodate new graduation requirements that necessitate students' taking more subjects. Schools have gone from eight to nine, and even from nine to ten periods.
- Some schools, having difficulty scheduling certain subjects within the school day, are adding "zero" periods and "afterschool" periods to meet their needs.
- Still others have added alternative/at-risk programs that usually start after the regular school day, but sometimes overlap the last two periods.

Hence, the number of periods is not quite as clear-cut as it used to be.

4. Number of Sessions

Once a variable only for city schools, this concern has spread to their suburban and rural counterparts. The issue is space. Can all students be housed during a single time span? If not, there are three alternatives:

- One is end-to-end split shifts (e.g., periods 1–6 and 7–12). This is tough, given the very early start for some and the very late finish for others, but it's out there.
- Overlapping sessions can also be used to ease overcrowding. For example, students go in three (or even more) shifts: 1–7, 2–8, 3–9. With staggered starting and stopping times and several lunch periods, the school building is at capacity virtually every second of the school day. We'll talk more about this type of scheduling below.
- Modified overlap means that some students start a period late (2) while some (usually seniors) end a period or two early (7 or 8).

Bottom line: Are all your students in the building from the opening to the closing bell? If not, you have some variation of session scheduling.

5. Overlap or "Swing" Periods

On the subject of sessions, certain classes taken by all four grades must be on a common, overlap, or "swing" period when all students are present. Chorus is an example. Imagine what would happen if freshmen arrive a period late, seniors leave a period early, and Chorus is placed the first or last period. If the period for Chorus is a conflict matrix decision, your choice is now *further* limited by the multigrade makeup of the class. The plot thickens.

6. Tallies by Grade

Later, we will map out which of the four grades are in the building during which periods to determine the placement of sections. You need to keep a watchful eye on who is in the building. Suppose only a few seniors stick around for the last period; then steer clear of that period for twelfth graders. Similarly, if fifth period happens to be a dedicated lunch period for sophomores, avoid putting tenth grade sections on that period. Much more on this subject below.

7. Full Schedules

These are philosophical questions to be decided:

- Is there a required number of subjects students must take?
- If so, does the number vary by grade?
- Is there a minimum number of periods that students must be in the building?
- Are all students required to have a lunch period?
- Are study halls used to fill gaps in the schedule?

8. Consecutive Period Scheduling

A related question is whether upperclassmen are permitted to take their required subjects consecutively and then leave, usually for a job. With this model, students are coming and going all the time. The other extreme is to require all students to be present from opening to closing bell. The relationship with transportation (busing) will have a major bearing on this decision.

9. Study Halls

This is a *major* philosophical consideration. Bring this issue back to your colleagues and/or scheduling committee. There are at least *seven* options:

- *No Study Halls.* Yours is an open campus, similar to a college; students are free to come and go as they choose.
- *Additional Courses.* All students have a full complement of classes. Gaps in their schedules? They must fill them with additional electives.
- *Early Dismissal.* Students take their required subjects—and then leave. Or, students arrive a period (or two) late and just take their required subjects in order.
- *Large-Group Study Halls.* Students are assigned to the auditorium or some other large-group area whenever they have a gap in their schedule. A study hall is scheduled for every period in the day. What about first and/or last period? Another decision for the scheduling committee. Why have students in the building at those times? Let them arrive late or leave early if they have no class. On the other hand, your busing may preclude having students arrive at any time other than for first period.
- *Supervised Study Halls.* Large-group study halls tend to become holding areas for students who do not have classes. Smaller study halls where the environment is more conducive to doing homework or studying can be scheduled. More than one section may be needed on some periods, based on demand.
- *Study Skills.* Study halls can become actual classes where note-taking, research, library skills, study techniques, and other skills are taught, particularly for ninth graders.
- *Extra Help.* In lieu of study halls, students can opt for extra help, tutoring, time in the library, time at the computer center, volunteer work in an office, and so forth, during gaps in their schedule. This option depends on the degree of freedom in your school.

10. Teacher Courses

The conflict matrix will identify potential *course* conflicts for students. But what about *teachers?* Suppose that zero conflicts come up for Dramatics and Public Speaking. It would make sense to place them on the same period, except that it's possible the same *teacher* is slated to teach both and they have to be scheduled on different periods. This matrix doesn't give us this information.

11. Teacher Session

Once limited to large schools on multisessions, this problem has spread. Teachers rotate among different sessions (early, middle, late, etc.) because some are more desirable. Suppose you dutifully use the conflict matrix to determine that a particular elective will be first period. Soon after, you discover that the teacher who always teaches this course is due for a turn on late session. You may be obligated to move the class to a later period to accommodate that teacher—or assign a different one for the coming year. If rotation of session is an issue, then learn the rules.

12. Administrative Duties

- Mr. Abel is needed for cafeteria duty the fifth period.
- Miss Jones is requested to serve her duty in the Attendance Office first period.
- Dr. Carson is wanted for the Deans' Office during the eighth period.

The problem? Using the conflict matrix, you have already assigned Mr. Abel to a fifth-period class, Miss Jones to a first-period class, and Dr. Carson to an eighth-period class. These are all singletons, and there will be a domino effect if you start changing them now to accommodate these requests. Get word out to fellow administrators that if they need teachers for certain periods, you need this information *before* you start scheduling. Let them scribble the information on a napkin. You must know when teachers are *un*available for classroom duties *before* you start assigning sections.

√ Helpful Hint 26

Write a short memo to your fellow administrators: "Speak now or forever hold your peace. I am beginning work on the construction of the master schedule. If you want specific teachers for specific administrative duties on specific periods, I need that information *immediately*. Once I assign them teaching periods, it will be impossible to make a change. Please review your needs and get back to me as soon as possible."

---

13. Department Capacity

As you start assigning sections, keep in mind the number of teachers per department. Don't put more classes on a period than there are teachers. Suppose period 2 is a problem because every student, Grades 9–12, is present because there is no lunch period then. Obviously, you need a section for every student. To load period 2, you create six business classes—but there are only five teachers.

14. Room Capacity

In the same vein, keep an eye on teaching spaces. In some well-endowed schools, each teacher has his or her own room. No problem there. But more often than not, space is at premium and teachers share rooms. As with department capacity, do not create more sections on a period than teaching spaces; otherwise, you will end up with classes in the balcony of the auditorium or the library.

15. Computer Rooms

This is becoming a growing problem as computer instruction expands. More departments are offering courses that require the use of computers. How many periods does your school have? How many courses require computers on a regular basis? Keep a watchful eye on this trend; don't schedule more computer classes than computer labs on a given period. How frequently are computer stations needed: Daily? Weekly? Less often? Sharing may be necessary. In Step 4, I referred to the elective Computer Graphics, doomed by a lack of computer facilities on a particular period. Set up a miniconflict matrix just for computer room utilization.

Another one of those miniconflict matrices would come in handy. As you build the schedule for all departments, keep track of those sections that require special facilities. For example, the matrix charts the placement of courses by periods that require the use of a computer lab. There are four separate computer labs in the building. You can see the importance of plotting out the usage. Where possible, a lab is dedicated to just one department, but there is considerable sharing. English, Social Studies, Math, Science, Language, Art, Business Education, and Special Education all require computer labs for their courses—and odds are the number of courses requiring a computer lab will continue to grow. Note how tight things are in this example. When you do this exercise on your own, you may discover that you have to shift a section or two because you have too many courses requiring a lab on a given period.

Computer Lab—Room Utilization by Course/Period

	1	2	3	4	5	6	7	8
Computer Lab 1	Keyboard	Accounting; Business Analysis		Keyboard	Conversational Spanish	Business Analysis; Recordkeeping	Special Education	Keyboard
Computer Lab 2	Computer Applications	Computer Applications	Computer Applications	Computer Applications	Computer Applications	Computer Applications	Computer Applications	Computer Applications
Computer Lab 3	Social Studies Research	Statistics	Science Projects	Conversational French	Journalism; Creative Writing	Science Projects	Social Studies Research	
Computer Lab 4	English Writing Lab	English Writing Lab	English Writing Lab	English Writing Lab	English Writing Lab	English Writing Lab	English Writing Lab	English Writing Lab

16. Specialized/Unique Rooms

Computer rooms are not the only specialized rooms that must be carefully scheduled. Let's return to those two English electives, Dramatics and Public Speaking. The conflict matrix showed zero student conflicts between the two. Furthermore, two different teachers were slated to teach them. It would seem that there was no reason not to place them on the same period. This time, however, it was the *room assignment* that was the problem. Both teachers requested the Little Theatre, a standard classroom redesigned for performance classes. With no *student* or *teacher* conflicts, we had forgotten about a possible *room* conflict and scheduled both electives for the same period. The teachers were irate, as well they should have been. By the time they found out, it was far too late to make a change. For one year, they shared the Little Theatre and a standard classroom.

17. Room Dovetailing

One more variable having to do with rooming. Reference was made to sharing, necessary where space limitations preclude each teacher from having his or her own room. Where sharing is unavoidable, make every effort to minimize the number of rooms to which a teacher is assigned by "dovetailing," as explained in the box below. Nobody likes to float.

√ Helpful Hint 28

Try the three-into-two model. For example: Here are the schedules of Teachers A and B: 1—3—4—6—8 and 2—4—5—7—8, respectively. Teacher C, the new kid on the block, may not have his own room, but can use the classrooms of Teachers A and B when they're empty: 1—2—5—6—7. It's certainly better than having three, four, or even five different classrooms.[2]

---

18. Teaming

I am a big proponent of teachers teaming together, but it is not always easy to connect two (or more) teachers at the expense of other variables. I will make the necessary accommodations in the schedule—as long as I am told about it in advance. If the information comes after I have started building the schedule, it is too late. All that I can say is, "Wait until next year." There are five types of teaming:

Intradisciplinary Teaming. Two teachers in the same department want their classes scheduled together on a particular period so that they can bring them together. For example, two Biology teachers want to schedule their classes at the same time so that they can do large-group/small-group instruction, depending on the unit. Such an arrangement is possible only in large schools in which there are multiple sections of core courses, enough so that you can place two on the same period. Otherwise, you may be creating potential conflicts. To have just four sections of a course—and then to place two of them on the same period—could prove troublesome.

---

[2] When I made this point at a workshop, one participant argued that room assignments should not be based on seniority. His felt that first-year teachers have enough problems and floating should not be one of them. If anything, he went on, they should be the first to have their own rooms. Try broaching this at a faculty meeting!

Interdisciplinary Teaming. In this case, two teachers in two *different* departments work together. For example, why should the French Revolution (Social Studies) and *A Tale of Two Cities* (English) be taught separately? They should be taught together—which is possible if the English and Social Studies teachers are paired. The concept of teaming was discussed earlier. There are several possible pairings to which it applies. Math and Science classes may also lend themselves to this kind of teaming.

Inclusion. The latest form of teaming involves inclusion; in most models it entails pairing a regular education with a Special Education teacher for coteaching. Not only do the teaching periods of the two teachers have to match, but there has to be common planning time for them as well. This can be extremely challenging, given other, competing demands placed on the scheduler.

Regrouping. Another variation of teaming involves putting several sections of the same course on the same period and then shuffling the students at the midyear point based on performance during the fall semester. This arrangement is similar to the intradisciplinary teaming just described—but its objectives are different. There are several highly beneficial advantages to this model, including pulling out the potential failures, putting the weakest students together, and letting the others proceed without being held back—at the beginning of the second semester. But there is also a major disadvantage in that a singleton class is artificially being created by putting all the sections on that one period, rather than spreading them over several. You will have to weigh the costs to see if the benefits accrued are worth it.

Push-Ins. A relatively new version of teaming involves "pushing in" a specialty teacher to regular classes. For example, a Fine Arts teacher is assigned a .2 to visit as many Social Studies classes as her own schedule permits to discuss the art history of the period the class is studying.

19. Paralleling

Suppose that students in the AP European Studies course want to drop down a level to the Social Studies 10 Honors class, but the two are not aligned. In other words, suppose the AP sections were assigned periods 4 and 7 while the Honors sections were 3 and 8. Students needing a change had to upset their entire schedule. Where possible, different levels of the same course should be put at the same time to facilitate schedule changes (assuming they are merited). If this can't be done for all the sections in all the courses, then try to do it for at least one or two. Some schedulers disagree, intentionally placing the courses on separate periods. With an irresolvable conflict, the student has a second chance, albeit with a different course. Another one for your scheduling committee to decide.

20. Half-Year Courses

So far, we've been concentrating on full-year courses. In building the schedule, place half-year sections so students will at least have a shot at flowing from a fall course to a spring course on the same period. It doesn't always work, but it's worth a try: Economics in the fall, Government in the spring . . . Oceanography—fall, Marine Biology—spring . . . and so forth. Look what can happen if you *don't* align courses. In an eight-period day, Ellen has six full-year courses and two-half year electives, plus lunch. If the semester-long courses are singletons on two different periods, her schedule will not work at midyear when the semester course changes periods. There is no place to go. Study the patterns (i.e., the half-year courses, which students tend to take in tandem). This comes with experience; after a while, you'll just know that Business Law students in the fall tend to become Business Analysis students in the spring. In Step 7, we'll see that pairing half-year courses is a common glitch in constructing a satisfactory schedule for each student.

√ Helpful Hint 29

As you become more sophisticated with the process, you will see that you can develop a conflict matrix for only those half-year courses. Rather than relying on intuition or guessing, you will be able to see which ones are paired, at least as far as student course requests are concerned. Then you can make more informed decisions with regard to placing them on common periods.

---

21. Part-Timers

Not all teachers teach a full five-class load. Suppose we need an additional section of a course and hire a .2 part timer. Teachers with other assignments (dean, department head, coordinator, etc.) may teach fewer than five. Before placing sections, find out when these individuals are available. It would be double work to assign them—only to find out that they are unavailable certain periods. I recall bringing back a Foreign Language teacher on child care leave to cover an additional section created because of increased enrollment. We just assumed that she would want first period. We assumed wrong; she was available only for an eighth period class. This was clearly our fault, and we had to make a change to accommodate her. The following year, we needed to hire an itinerant teacher to teach a lone section of Japanese. You can be sure we checked her availability before placing that section!

22. Shared Staff

The most common sharing is between high schools and middle schools, although there are other arrangements as well: A Science teacher who could handle AP Chemistry was shared between two districts; a French teacher's schedule was divided among three districts because there were not enough classes in any one to sustain a full-time position. Whatever the sharing plan, work out in advance when this person is assigned to your school, generally "morning" versus "afternoon." With a five-class teacher, usually the school that has the person three-fifths makes the determination, unless there is some special need the other school has. Communications is key.

√ Helpful Hint 30

Before the scheduling process begins, it might be a wise idea to hold a conference committee meeting between the two (or more schools) involved in any sharing of staff or students. In this way, any bugs could be ironed out before separate schedules are built. An unexpected dividend of this meeting might be the discovery that one building has a surplus where the other has a deficit, and some additional sharing could be arranged.

23. Lunch Periods

Make sure every teacher has an official lunch period—when the cafeteria is open and food is served.[3] I recall a situation in which a teacher was assigned periods 1-2-5-6-7. He was told that he could eat fourth or eighth period. The problem was that the lunchroom was open only periods 5, 6, and 7. He didn't object to the fact that food wasn't served, but that he would have nobody to eat with. A legitimate concern. In some districts, a *contractual* concern. Sometimes a teacher may *voluntarily* take an oddball lunch period to accommodate unique scheduling requests.

24. Vocational Education

Theoretically, potential problems should appear via the conflict matrix. But that doesn't always happen. Vocational Education is delivered in a variety of ways by different school districts, let alone different states. The situation below is applicable to all and makes the point. Let me begin with some generalizations:

- Vocational Education is usually a multiperiod program, sometimes as many as four periods in duration: for example—1–4 (morning) or 5–8 (afternoon).
- Generally eleventh and twelfth graders take Vocational Education, although there are exceptions. Some schools send a few students to all-day programs.
- Often these programs are at a site other than the main campus of the high school. Sometimes they are a considerable distance away.

With these givens in mind, follow this scenario. A part-time teacher to cover three sections of General Biology was hired. It was agreed she would teach three periods in a row: 1–2–3. Biology is usually taken during the sophomore year. What we didn't take into account was that most Vocational Education students are juniors and seniors who have gone this route after encountering difficulty with academic courses. A disproportionate number had failed General Biology and were now repeating it. When it came time to schedule their courses, those attending morning (periods 1–4) Vocational Education faced an irresolvable conflict with the three sections of the General Biology course running 1–2-3. A fourth section had to be created during an afternoon period to accommodate these students.

25. Inclusion

This relatively new strand of Special Education was alluded to in the section above on "teaming," but it merits a separate discussion. There are many models; three will be mentioned here.

- One is the *block program,* whereby a group of inclusion students travels together for their core subjects (English-Social Studies-Math-Science) in regular education classes, accompanied by a Special Education teacher, who then meets alone with them during the last period to review the day's work. This model is relatively easy to schedule. Determine which regular education sections are designated "inclusion" and reserve seats for the inclusion students who will be joining those classes. "Cap"

---

[3]When I mention this concern during the workshop, I invariably get a laugh: A closed cafeteria may or not be an advantage, depending on the food that is served!

them lower when we get to Step 8 and load the sections. First, you have to reserve seats for the inclusion students; second, these classes should ideally be a speck smaller, given the dual set of demands on the teacher. Finding some common planning time for the Special Education teacher and these four regular education teachers is also beneficial, but maybe difficult to do, at least for all of them together at one time.

- The second model, used as an example above, involves *coteaching*. Certain regular education sections need to be earmarked as inclusion. The caps on these sections must be set correspondingly lower. The hard part comes when the teaching schedules have to be coordinated to allow not only team teaching, but common prep time as well.

- For districts that are struggling with financial concerns, a *push-in* model is also possible, whereby a Special Education teacher is not dedicated to any one section, but covers several over the course of a week. Obviously, the support is more limited.

26. Personnel Decisions

So far, most decisions have been fairly mechanical, made by crunching numbers. Now, a *human* element will be added. In reviewing the tallies for Business Education, the number of sections decreased for next year by one, from fifteen to fourteen. It was clear-cut; that loss of a .2 was justified, but that's not the end of the story. The school had made a concerted effort to build up its Business program and had recruited three dynamos. The third, the least senior, was the biggest superstar of all. Now his position was to be reduced from five to four classes, making him part-time (.8). The administration knew that he wouldn't stick around with a 20 percent cut. Other districts would scoop him up in a nanosecond. What would happen the following year, if the number of sections went back up to fifteen (or more)? This could be a temporary blip. Hence, the scheduler found a fifteenth section to restore him to full-time status. Possibilities included adding a section of a multisection course (such as Keyboarding), restoring an elective originally cut, or creating a Business elective for Special Education students.[4] This is the perfect time to point out that sections don't magically add up to multiples of five. There is more flexibility for large departments with many teachers and sections, but trickier for smaller ones, which are particularly sensitive to lower numbers.

27. Teacher Requests

This is a tough one. Above, I provided a sample preference sheet for teachers. We get into an age-old debate: Are high-powered (AP, honors, electives, upperclass) courses assigned based on seniority? Or, should there be rotation, with each teacher getting a fair share of the best classes? No easy answer. Some believe that the rookies have to pay their dues, taking the least desirable classes at first. "We all did that," veterans point out. But others believe that top classes should be rotated among everyone. Still others, the compromisers, maintain that all teachers should be given a balanced program with at least one top pick. Tradition and the culture in your

---

[4] Notice that I didn't mention having him teaching the fifth class out of license in another department. This option is patently illegal in many states where teachers must teach all of their classes in their certification areas. Check your own state/district regs in this area if you are considering such a move.

school will determine which way you go. These policies may even vary from department to department in the same building. There should be a discussion of this policy at a faculty or department meeting, or by the scheduling committee.

Class assignments are not the only preferences. Teachers often request certain lunch periods, preparation periods, duties, classrooms, and even the configurations of their teaching schedules. Should you consider these in building the schedule?

As I said, personalized requests run the gamut:

- Can I have first period off? What about last period off?
- Can I have most of my classes in the morning?
- Can you give me my two Spanish 2 classes back to back?
- Can you make sure not to give me more than two classes in a row?
- Can Mildred and I have the same lunch period? Can it be fifth period?
- Can I have my own classroom—not too far from the restroom?

√ Helpful Hint 31

Whatever you decide, you must be perfectly open about your policy. Again, there are few secrets in a school. To state that you don't honor requests—and then year after year two of your cronies end up with the preferred lunch period and being free the last period of the day will not sit well with the faculty. Favoritism is the best way to undermine your credibility and alienate the staff. If you do for one, do for everyone.

You get the idea. To repeat: What you do for one, you do for all.[5]

Follow this scenario. Six Technology teachers made the following request: Could they all have the last period of the day as their "prep" period to clean up and close down their shops? A legitimate request, given the unique nature of their work—but not practical. I empathized, but explained that from the standpoint of scheduling, it was unwise not to run *any* Technology classes on any one period. Then I offered a compromise: a three-year rotation during which two of the six would have the last period as a prep period each year. While not ideal, it was better than nothing. I had accomplished three objectives: First, I had said "No," but "No—with a reason," a parenting trick that works in other situations as well. Second, at least I offered something; it wasn't a flat-out rejection of a legitimate concern. Third, that deal was equitable for all six. I could have said, "No—this will not work." Then, when the schedule came out, my pal always seemed to get that last period off. Nothing could be more transparent to a faculty, and nothing can do more to kill morale. In the book's Introduction I listed the three skills that every administrator needs. Remember: technical, conceptual, and interpersonal. Handling teacher requests falls into the third.

---

[5] Principals will recognize the following scene which takes places on opening day. Teaches report to the auditorium for the opening faculty meeting. The master schedule has just been given out. The principal looks out at his audience. The teachers are not looking at him; they are analyzing the schedule. But they're not studying what they have; they're more interested in what everyone else has.

28. Common Planning Time

Common planning time or C.P.T. has become a priority on wish lists. As collaboration within departments, between departments, and with Special Education increases, so does the need for planning time. Another trend is to break large schools down into "units" or "houses"; once again, teachers need time outside the classroom to share. In one model, core teachers in a middle school all had first period off; while they were free, their students took Physical Education or electives. This was called the "breakfast period" for the teachers, but a great deal more was accomplished than enjoying coffee and bagels. It gave staff members a chance to compare notes, plan lessons, and discuss students' progress. If it was reported that Jimmy was having trouble in English, then other teachers could indicate if his work was suddenly deteriorating in their classes as well. Although most of the planning time was informal, the information gleaned from these sessions—not to mention the team-building, bonding, and camaraderie—was invaluable.

> **√ Helpful Hint 32**
>
> When report cards were given out, the core teachers met as a committee, and over a week's time invited the students in the program to come and talk with the group about their progress. Parents were also invited to be present for these sessions.

29. Accommodations

You may have staff members with documented disabilities who require accommodations, usually with regard to classrooms and facilities. Make sure you are cognizant of their needs as you start to build the schedule.

30. The Mad Dash

Last, and least, in terms of priority and doability, is what I call the mad dash. It's easier to illustrate than explain. Suppose there are two Technology shops, one at each of the opposite ends of your building. I don't know of any contract that prohibits your scheduling a Tech teacher as follows: first period—Shop A; second period—Shop B; third period—Shop A; fourth period—off; fifth period—Shop B, and so on. The only thing this scheduling will accomplish is strong legs and maybe a retirement incentive. Where facilities are concerned, some attention should be paid to clustering classes together. For example: If the teacher is scheduled for two Auto classes in one shop, two Wood classes in a second, and an Electricity shop in a third, make every effort to keep those classes together so as to minimize opening and closing several times a day. A similar case involved a Physical Education teacher who taught two classes in the gym, two at the swimming pool, and one Health Education section in a standard classroom. Every effort was made to prevent her from running all over the building.

I often get this follow-up question: What about scheduling different levels of the same subject? For example, would the following be acceptable? First period—English 12; second period—English 9; fourth period—back to an English 12, and so on. Definitely. Teachers may prefer having the same levels back to back, particularly convenient when they are giving tests, but it is virtually impossible to factor this variable into the scheduling. The one exception might be Foreign

Language. Take a teacher who is trilingual; it is difficult to shift gears among French, Spanish, and Italian several times a day.

Recap

So there you have it: *thirty factors* to consider as you start to build the master schedule. Yes, some are far more critical than others, but they all must be considered. After completing the list, I usually get a sigh of relief from my workshop participants who heretofore had no clue as to how much thought went into placing each and every section. One comment stuck with me: "You have to juggle all those balls at once."

Methods for Building

By now you're anxious to get going; so where do you begin? We need to look at some of the methods experienced schedulers have used in placing sections. Size counts. There is definitely a correlation between the size of the student population and the method used. Also, we need to say something about the supplies my colleagues use. I have seen everything from magnetic boards to graph paper, index cards to magnets. I am not going to say which is best; use whatever works for you. Here are four frequently used methods for constructing a master schedule:

Method 1—Small Schools

With a school under 500, the task can be constructed centrally, once the parameters have been established. Look at the following master schedule for a ninth grade center with 360 students:

		1	2	3	4	5	6	7	8	9	10
English 9R	10	X	X	X	X	X	X	X	X	X	X
English 9S	2		X		X						
Social Studies 9	12	X	X	XX	X	X	X	XX	X	X	X
Math 9R	9		X	X	X	X	X	X	X	X	X
Math 9S	2							X	X		
Math 10	1								X		
Earth Science R	8		X	X	X	X	X	X	X	X	
Earth Science S	3		X	X		X					
Biology	1						X				
Spanish	6			X	X	X		X	X	X	
French	4			X	X		X		X		
Italian	2						X		X		

(Continued)

(Continued)

		1	2	3	4	5	6	7	8	9	10
Art	7	X	X		X	X		X	X	X	
Music	5		X	X			X		X	X	
Physical Education	11	X	X	X	XX	X	X	X	X	X	X
Team Sports	1			X							
TOTAL	**84**	**4**	**8**	**12**	**9**	**9**	**9**	**9**	**12**	**8**	**4**

Study this schedule carefully. There is a great deal to be learned from its construction:

1. As already noted, there are 360 students in this school.

2. The average class size is thirty.

3. There are two "tracks" for certain subjects: "Regular" for academic students; "Skills" for weaker students.

4. All students take seven subjects:
   - English 9—Regular or Skills
   - Social Studies 9 (heterogeneous)
   - Math 9—Regular or Skills—or Math 10 (for accelerated students)
   - Earth Science 9—Regular or Skills—or Biology (for accelerated students)
   - Spanish or French or Italian
   - Art or Music (choice of elective)
   - Physical Education (except for student athletes taking Team Sports)

5. The students are on three sessions, with a third of them on each: periods 1–8, 2–9, 3–10.

6. There are three singletons—and they have been placed on different periods. Also note that none has been placed on periods 1, 2, 9, or 10—because not all of the students are in the building at those times. Remember what we said above about placing certain singletons on swing periods when all students are present: Math 10 (8th), Biology (6th), and Team Sports (3rd).

7. The Skills classes, although not singletons, have been placed on different periods to facilitate scheduling.

8. English 9R was one of the easiest courses to schedule: ten sections, ten periods.

9. Both Social Studies and Physical Education have more sections than there are periods—so there are two sections of both courses on certain periods. There is tremendous flexibility as to where to place those sections; put them on periods where you need a place to absorb students. This concept is explained below.

10. Art and Music are spread out over nine of the ten periods; neither teacher was available tenth period—otherwise, a section would have been placed on that period, too.

11. There are four lunch periods: 4, 5, 6, and 7. Hence, there are fewer sections on those periods—since fewer students are available to take classes at those times.

12. Most important: Look at the total number of sections per period at the bottom of each of the columns:
    - Start with periods 3 and 8; during those two periods, all 360 students are in the building. Given thirty in a class, that means you need a total of *twelve* sections.
    - Look at periods 1 and 10; only a third of the students are in the building, as just explained. Hence 120 students (1/3 of 360) require *four* sections, given thirty per class.
    - Look at periods 2 and 9; two thirds of the students are in the building, also as explained above. You need *eight* sections during those periods.
    - Look at the lunch periods; all of the students are in the building—but one quarter of them are at lunch each period:

    Hence, one fourth of 360 = 90.

    And, 360 minus 90 = 270.

    Finally, 270 divided by 30 = 9.

It is critical that you understand how the number of sections per period was determined. Suppose you had arbitrarily put six sections on period 1, not having gone through this exercise. Don't be surprised if those sections ended up small in size; there just weren't enough students to fill them. On the other hand, suppose you had arbitrarily put ten sections on period 3. Conversely, there would not have been enough room to absorb all 360 students: 360 divided by 10 = 36. Remember what I said above about Social Studies and Physical Education: You had the luxury of placing two sections on some periods. As you build your master, look at which period(s) you need to build up with more sections and place them there. Think of them as wild cards. However, if by this point you've already put four sections on period 1 or 10, you're certainly not going to place one of those wild cards on those periods; why would you? We will return to the critical issue of sections-per-periods in the section titled "Juggling These Variables," below.

Method 2—Middle-Size Schools

In the second method, the master scheduler centrally builds—but in concert with the department heads. He still keeps a watchful eye on the total number of sections per period as a schedule is developed for each department. The variables enumerated in the section above are all taken into account as teachers are assigned and sections are placed. Follow this scenario:

The following program/load has been carved out for Mrs. Andrews:

(2) English 10 Honors

(2) English 10 College Prep

(1) Creative Writing in the Fall and (1) Creative Writing in the Spring

This makes a total of *five* sections. To what periods should these courses be assigned?

- Two sections of Social Studies 10 Honors have *tentatively* been assigned to periods 1 and 5.

- Two periods of Math 10 Honors have *tentatively* been assigned to periods 3 and 6.
- Assuming that many of the same students are taking English 10 Honors, it's a no-brainer to assign them to periods other than 1–3–5–6. The conflict matrix can verify this information. For now, we'll arbitrarily schedule those two sections of English 10 Honors for Mrs. Andrews to periods 2 and 7. Note that I said "for now"; this is subject to change if things don't work out in the end. Similarly, the periods *tentatively* assigned for the Social Studies and Math Honors classes could also change later as well.
- Now it's time to assign the two sections of English 10 R. Quite a few have already been *tentatively* assigned to other teachers for periods 3, 5, 7, and 8. Let's put Mrs. Andrews's sections on different periods. She's already been *tentatively* scheduled for those Honors sections on periods 2 and 7. So, let's give her the two Regular classes on periods 1 and 4. As of now, she is teaching periods 1, 2, 4, and 7.
- Now we're left with the two half-year sections of Creative Writing. It would be wise to split them, using two different periods. In effect, you are turning a singleton into a doubleton and enabling more students to fit this elective into their schedule. Referring to the conflict matrix, periods 1, 2, 6, 7, and 8 are possibilities. You could change one of the four classes already penciled in for Mrs. Andrews, but you don't have to, at least at this point. Periods 1, 2, and 7 have already been used, but periods 6 and 8 have not. Hence, we'll place Creative Writing on period 6 in the fall . . . and period 8 in the spring.
- Mrs. Andrews schedule is *tentatively* set:

First period	—	English 10 Regular
Second period	—	English 10 Honors
Fourth period	—	English 10 Regular
Sixth period	—	Creative Writing (Fall)
Seventh period	—	English 10 Honors
Eighth period	—	Creative Writing (Spring)

- I keep saying *tentatively*. Many things may come up in later steps that would necessitate adjusting the periods. For example, one of those periods might not load well; or, there could be additional conflicts that went undetected, necessitating a change; or, there might be too many sections on one of those periods, forcing a change. We'll go into far greater detail in Step 7, but for the time being, Mrs. Andrews's schedule is done.

Method 3—Large Schools

Which came first, the chicken or the egg? Which comes first, the teacher or the period? In large schools, the scheduler may build a master without taking teachers into account. Conflicts can be avoided, periods can be spread to best advantage, and the number of sections per period can be monitored. He gives the list to the department head, who carves out a schedule for each teacher:

French 1 periods 3, 7, 9

French 2 periods 1, 2, 4, 5, 9

French 3 periods 1, 2, 4, 6, 7, 8, 9

Spanish 1 periods 1, 7, 9

Spanish 2 periods 1, 2, 3, 4, 6

Spanish 3 periods 5, 8

√ Helpful Hint 33

Most schedulers use a scheduling board of some sort to complete the assignment: For example, a magnetic board with a scheduling grid is one way to go. The teacher's names are written in the row heads and the list of courses to be assigned is written on magnetic strips. As classes are assigned, they come off the pile and onto the board. A similar arrangement involves using a notebook with pockets (called a Delaney book). Each section is placed on a small card. The notebook has to have the same number of pockets as there are periods. As a section is placed, a card goes into one of the pockets. Either way, the finished product starts to look something like this, using the French and Spanish classes just listed above:

Period/ teacher	1st	2nd	3rd	4th	5th	6th	7th	8th	9th
Ames	French 2	French 2	French 1		French 2				French 1
Barker	French 3			French 2		French 3	French 1		French 2
Cox	Spanish 2	Spanish 2			Spanish 3	Spanish 2		Spanish 3	
Dwyer		French 3		French 3			French 3	French 3	French 3
Evans	Spanish 1		Spanish 2	Spanish 2			Spanish 1		Spanish 1

Method 4—Computer Generated

There is a growing trend to let the computer do the work for you. Some scheduling software packages have sophisticated programs that actually place the sections. While they vary considerably, they all begin by asking the scheduler to answer basic questions about each and every course. For example:

- Earliest starting period and latest possible finishing period
- Teacher(s) available to teach this course
- Room considerations as well as special facilities needed
- Teachers' ability/availability to teach every course/period

Once these questions have been answered for each and every course, the computer will find the best possible period to place those classes to ensure that the maximum number of students can fit it into those sections. Teacher schedules are then constructed. Some schedulers swear by this method, convinced that the computer makes the best possible choices. Others prefer to build by hand, taking into account human considerations, which the computer doesn't handle.

Juggling These Variables

Before attempting some exercises to put into practice what has been presented, let's look at some of the many variables that must be juggled simultaneously. These apply regardless of which of the above-mentioned methods is employed. I have excerpted sections of an article I distributed to the faculty the day the master schedule was released. The staff didn't comprehend how much thought went into the placement of each and every section, and I became frustrated with requests for moving a section after the schedule had been posted. I've come to call my response the domino effect, because even the slightest change can cause a chain reaction affecting many other sections, not only in that department, but in others as well.

To illustrate, I use Social Studies schedule as an example because it is relatively the easiest to schedule for three reasons: First, it has the most multisection courses; second, it has relatively few electives; and third, it has no lab classes[6]—three variables that make scheduling all the easier. On the downside, the placement of sections is complicated by the fact that other departments may have been scheduled and locked by the time Social Studies is reached, thereby limiting the degree of choice.

Let's take a goldfish-bowl look at how these scheduling decisions are made and some of the factors that must be juggled simultaneously as the Social Studies department schedule is constructed.

1. Every effort is made to spread R (Regular)-level courses with one section on as many different periods as possible.

2. Skills-level classes, far fewer in number, must be balanced between morning and afternoon to accommodate Vocational Education students, who leave the high school campus for either the morning or the afternoon.

3. However, an eye must be kept on keeping Skills-level classes parallel (as much as possible) with R-level courses to facilitate mobility between levels.

4. Skills-level class placements are also dictated by where Skills-level classes have already been placed in other departments so as to minimize conflicts.

5. The conflict matrix must be consulted to minimize conflicts with all electives.

6. Advanced Placement courses in European Studies and American Studies are also governed by the conflict matrix.

7. Honors classes should parallel the AP sections, in the event that students need to change levels once the school year has begun.

8. Some schools offer "extra help" classes in Social Studies. These should be placed on lunch periods, when students can best take advantage of them.

9. Teacher assignments also "wag the dog." For example, if a highly specialized elective continues to be sixth period, then that placement will have a bearing on when that teacher's other classes are scheduled. In other words, sixth period is now out of the mix for this particular teacher. This decision alone can have a domino effect, as we shall see.

---

[6] Some schools now give weaker students alternate day "lab" classes in Social Studies. Sometimes, these period-and-a-half classes dovetail with the same scheduling pattern in English. For example, a student would have English period 4, Social Studies period 6—and an alternate day lab in English or Social Studies on period 5.

10. Special administrative assignments (bus duty, lunch duty, attendance office, etc.) also affect teachers' schedules and course placements.

11. Now, as if things weren't complicated enough, teaming of teachers has to be considered. There may be requests for intra- and interdisciplinary scheduling. For example, two teachers in Social Studies may want to work together with a common pool of students. Or, there may be teaming between Social Studies and English, whereby courses are taught in an interdisciplinary manner. One such model involves a double period, say periods 3 and 4. Both the English and Social Studies teachers have back-to-back classes. The same students are assigned to both teachers. The students who have English third period go as a block to the Social Studies teacher fourth period. It's vice versa for the students who have Social Studies third period. Sections can be combined in a variety of ways to permit the integration of the two subjects.

12. Part-time and shared teachers' schedules must be considered. There may be a teacher split between two buildings (high school and middle school, or two high schools in the district). Similarly, there may be a part-timer teaching fewer than five classes, and his availability must be taken into account.

13. As if things are not complex enough, room assignments must be considered when placing sections. Not only do we have to make sure there is a room for every section, particularly on peak load periods when the building may be at capacity, but we should make every effort to minimize floating for teachers who do not have the same room for the entire day. This is accomplished by dovetailing schedules as much as possible, as described above.

14. Certain classes have special room or facilities needs, so room utilization becomes an added factor in the decision-making process. Computer classrooms, laboratories, and art rooms are but three examples. The demand for computer labs is far outpacing their availability. Some schools now have computers, or at least computer pods, in every classroom.

It cannot be emphasized enough that none of these fourteen factors operates in a vacuum; they all interact with one another simultaneously. We are juggling all of these variables all of the time. The following case study about assigning eight "regular" twelfth grade Social Studies classes drives home the point dramatically.

Teacher A will be teaching two Regular classes, two Honors classes, and one Skills-level class. The placement of the Skills class is dictated by the Vocational Education schedule. The placement of the Honors classes is affected by the conflict matrix, AP classes, and a request for teaming from an English teacher, who wants to do some interdisciplinary work. In addition, the Regular classes must be scheduled at different periods from those already assigned to Teacher B, who also has two Regular classes and is also teaching two twelfth-grade Economics classes—which must be paired with two twelfth-grade Government classes and an extra-help class that has to be offered during a lunch period. Teacher C also teaches two Regular classes, but then leaves for another school where she is assigned afternoon classes, so she must teach those two sections in the morning. Teacher D teaches the two remaining Regular classes, but is an assistant dean, and that governs her teaching schedule. For her third class, she teaches a popular elective that must be ninth period, and that further limits the placement of those two Regular classes.

As we conclude this section, then, you should see that the movement of a single section can affect classes up and down the line, not only in Social Studies, but in other departments as well. By now you are aware of all the factors that must be juggled . . . how they impinge upon one another . . . and how delicate the master schedule is.

Placing Sections

Many years ago when I presented these four alternatives for building the master schedule, a participant suggested a fifth. He said that in his school, each department head constructed the master schedule himself. Assuming he misunderstood, I suggested that the department heads carved out the course loads for each teacher and maybe even had some input as to the periods, particularly singletons. "No," he persisted. "Each department head decided the periods for each of his teachers."

This remark produced a dead silence. A bit startled, I countered with a question: Suppose the department head wanted to give his teachers very few first periods . . . very few last periods . . . the same lunch . . . and common preparation periods. Where would the students go when all those teachers weren't teaching? Now, to compound matters—imagine if all the other department heads did the same thing. What would be the end result? There would be too many sections on some periods and not enough on others. The other workshop participants understood that there has to be a formal procedure for establishing how many sections are offered each period of the day.

Once we achieved consensus on this fundamental point, I asked the group how many sections there should be on each period. Without thinking, one participant blurted out: "Obviously—the same number." Fortunately, another saw the error of her thinking: What about students who don't have a first period? Or, students who don't have a last period? What about lunch periods? The participants were starting to see what I have come to call "the curve of the school." Let's return to the master schedule I used above as a model and look at the number of sections per period:

1st	2nd	3rd	4th	5th	6th	7th	8th	9th	10th
4	8	12	9	9	9	9	12	8	4

Just by inspection, you should be able to see the curve of the school:

- Only four sections are required for first and tenth periods because only one third of the students are present.
- Only eight sections are required second and ninth because only two thirds of the students are present.
- Only nine sections are required periods 4, 5, 6, and 7 because these are lunch periods and one fourth of the students are out of classes during each of these four periods.
- A full complement (12 sections) is required for third and eighth periods because *all* of the students are in the building and in classes.

Group members seem to grasp this concept. However, invariably I get this question: Not every class is the same size; then what happens? For example, Physical

Education classes may be larger . . . Special Education classes smaller. There are other courses (Art, Technology, Computer, etc.) with unique class sizes. Good observation and definitely true, but things balance out—and the curve concept is at least a starting point for plotting sections. In Step 7, we will see how further adjustments may have to be made to compensate for that variability in section size.

Exercise

Try this exercise to plot the number of sections needed per period. It must be underscored that this is not perfect—but it's certainly better than randomly deciding that number, ending up with too many on some, and too few on others. Failure to make these projections can result in overcrowding at some times of the day and underutilization at others. Look at the ten givens listed below and then fill in the grid. You might view this as one of those popular logic puzzles. Note: There is only one solution.

1. This school has 1,200 students. There are 300 students in each grade, 9–12.
2. The average section size is thirty. Hence, when the entire grade is in the building and taking classes, there are ten sections: 300 divided by 30 = 10.
3. Not all students arrive for first period: 10 percent of the students in each of the four grades do *not* have a first period. How many sections do you need? (9 × 4 = 36)
4. *All* ninth graders have lunch during period 4. What would happen if you placed a ninth grade class on period 4? The answer is obvious.
5. *All* tenth graders have lunch during period 5.
6. *All* eleventh graders have lunch during period 6.
7. Half of the eleventh graders don't have an eighth period class; they leave early.
8. *No* senior has an eighth period class; they all leave early.
9. Half of the twelfth graders don't have a seventh period class.
10. One fifth of twelfth graders don't have a sixth period class; they have their five subjects in a row and then leave the building. Don't worry about lunch for seniors.

Using the information above and the chart below, determine how many sections will be needed each period.

Don't know where to start? Begin with the no-brainers; put a zero for the ninth, tenth, and eleventh grade lunch periods; put a zero for the seniors on eighth period. Think back to the jigsaw puzzle analogy explained above. Where did you begin? With the corners. Well, in this case, the givens are the corners.

	1	2	3	4	5	6	7	8	Total
9th									
10th									
11th									
12th									
Total									

Explanation

1. Remember what we said about there being ten sections per grade when the entire grade is in class. If 10 percent of the students in each of the four grades do not have a first period class, then you need nine sections for each. Enter 9–9–9–9.

2. Make sure you've put in those zeroes for lunch: fourth period for ninth graders . . . fifth period for tenth graders . . . sixth period for eleventh graders.

3. Since half of the eleventh graders don't have an eighth period class, you need five sections instead of ten.

4. Since no twelfth grader has an eighth period class, enter a zero.

5. Since half of the twelfth graders don't have a seventh period class, you need five sections instead of ten.

6. And, since one fifth (1/5 or 20%) of the twelfth graders don't have a sixth period class, you need eight sections instead of ten sections (1/5 of 10 = 2; 10 − 2 = 8).

7. For all of the other periods for each of the four grades, all the students are in class. Hence, you need ten sections.

This is what the finished grid should look like:

	1	2	3	4	5	6	7	8	Total
9th	9	10	10	0	10	10	10	10	69
10th	9	10	10	10	0	10	10	10	69
11th	9	10	10	10	10	0	10	5	64
12th	9	10	10	10	10	8	5	0	62
Total	36	40	40	30	30	28	35	25	264

As with the example above, it's the bottom row that reflects the curve of the school.

Let's look at it separately and draw some conclusions:

- The greatest number of sections is needed for second and third periods; students in all four grades are in class.
- The number of sections needed begins to tail off toward the end of the day as eleventh and twelfth graders start to leave early.
- The need for sections is slightly less on first period because some students in all four grades start their day with second period.
- Finally, the need for sections on the lunch periods is also correspondingly lower.
- In summary, this is the curve for this particular school.
- We saw a very different curve reflected in the master schedule for that small school of 360 students.
- The curve for a school in which all the students start and stop at the same time would be still different.
- Imagine a school with just one lunch period, or with two, or with five.

- Consider the curve for a school in which 20 percent of the students attend off-campus programs in the afternoon.
- Think about the problems faced in an already crowded building on the periods when all students are present at once and there are no lunch periods.

By now I hope you see the value of the curve and how vital it is to plot out the need for sections per period.

Adding People to the Mix

So far, the exercises have involved numbers and been fairly mechanical. Now we're ready to add personnel to the equation. The following exercise requires you to build the department program for six Technology teachers. Like the exercise just completed, there are certain givens that provide a good starting point; remember—the corners of the jigsaw puzzle. *Unlike* that exercise, there is more than one solution. As a matter of fact, there are many. First, look at the course load for each teacher; where a period is already indicated in bold, consider it a given, set by the conflict matrix. Second, review the guidelines for completing this task. Third, familiarize yourself with the scheduling grid to be used—and then get started.

Teachers/Courses	1st	2nd	3rd	Notes
Adams	(3) Auto 1	(2) Auto 2		
Carter	(3) Wood 1	(1) Wood 2—**4th**	(1) Wood 3—**2nd**	
Jackson	(2) Metal 1	(2) Elect 1	(1) Elect 2—**4th**	See note below
Lincoln (.6 FTE)	(3) Wood I			3 periods in a row
Madison	(2) Wood 1	(1) Robotics—**7th**	(2) Auto 1	Auto classes on consecutive periods
Tyler	(3) Graphics 1	(1) Graphics 2—**1st**	(1) Graphics 3—**8th**	Cannot teach 7th

Guidelines: Follow these steps in constructing the schedule for Technology:

1. As with the previous exercises, fill in the givens first, the corners of the puzzle. This will also limit your degree of choice for other decisions.

2. Use two writing instruments: red pen for the sections that are locked (the singletons, for example); pencil for everything else (subject to change).

3. The singleton period assignments cannot be changed.

4. Period 5 is a common lunch period used for planning time for all teachers in the department. No classes are to be scheduled on period 5. Get out the red pen.

5. Teachers cannot teach more than three periods in a row; teaching periods 3, 4, and 6 is OK.

6. There is only one Auto shop; therefore, only one Auto class can be scheduled per period. Hint: There are seven auto classes and seven periods.

7. Here's the tricky part: Jackson's (2) Electricity 1 sections must be at the same time as the Auto 1 sections of any other teacher—so there can be some team teaching.

8. There are two Wood shops, but try to spread the classes as much as possible.

9. Try to avoid having teachers run back and forth between two different shops.

10. Develop your own shorthand. Wood 1 can be W1, Graphics 3 can be G3, Electricity 2 can be E2. You will save time and make fewer errors this way.

	1	2	3	4	5	6	7	8
Adams								
Carter								
Jackson								
Lincoln								
Madison								
Tyler								

Carefully review your work to make sure you have followed all the guidelines:

- Does each of the teachers have the correct number of classes?
- Does each teacher have no more than three periods in a row?
- Are the singletons on the correct periods?
- Is there only one Auto class per period?
- Has the team teaching between Auto and Electricity been established?
- Have you attempted to spread the Wood 1 classes as much as possible?
- Have you followed the special notes for Jackson, Lincoln, Madison, and Tyler in the course load table?

Below is one possible solution—just one of many. Yours may be just as good. Singletons are **bolded** and the sections requiring special considerations are underlined:

	1	2	3	4	5	6	7	8
Adams	A1			A2	X	A2	<u>A1</u>	<u>A1</u>
Carter		**W3**	W1	**W2**	X		W1	W1
Jackson	M1	M1		**E2**	X		<u>E1</u>	<u>E1</u>
Lincoln	X	<u>W1</u>	<u>W1</u>	<u>W1</u>	X	X	X	X
Madison	W1	<u>A1</u>	<u>A1</u>		X	W1	**R1**	
Tyler	**G2**	G1	G1			G1	X	**G3**

Last word: Nothing was said about the number of sections per period, because that was not one of the givens. But as you can see, they are all fairly balanced. In addition, the wisdom of not offering any classes on period 5 can be debated. On the one hand, it obviously will make scheduling the students slightly harder, because you're taking one period out of circulation. On the other hand, the benefits accrued from the department's having common preparation time may make the sacrifice well worth it.

Notification of Teachers

Most districts are required to notify teachers of their course loads and/or actual teaching schedules for the following year. Usually, this comes sometime before the end of the current school year. Step 6 usually takes place in the early spring; we still must complete Step 7 before the master schedule is locked. Nevertheless, a sample letter is included here. The words can be adapted to meet your own situation and requirements:

√ Helpful Hint 34

Use this memo for formally notifying teachers of their assignments for the coming year. You may have to notify teachers of their (1) courses, (2) periods, and (3) other assignments.

OFFICE OF THE PRINCIPAL

To: _____

From: _____, Principal

Date: _____

As of this date, your course load/schedule for the next school year is as follows:

Please remember: Assignments are "tentatively definite"—and "definitely tentative"—pending any last-minute enrollment shifts and staffing changes.

_____

_____

_____

_____

Principal and Department Head's Signatures

[Note: You may have to show only the course load, or you may have to indicate the periods as well, or you may also have to include any other assignments, such as homeroom, duties, assigned lunch period, and so on. It depends on your teacher contract.]

Building a Large Department Schedule on Your Own

Now, as we get ready to complete Step 6, I'll offer the yeoman test: The construction of the Social Studies department schedule for a large school. There are thirteen teachers, with special considerations (and requests) for each one. This is the granddaddy of them all. I have built in plot twists and turns requiring you not only to put to use what you've learned so far, but also to make some judgment calls. The good news is that the periods have been determined; the bad news is that there is a great degree of choice, so you're going to have to give considerable thought to the placement of each and every section. Simply put: I've included just about every type of complication that I have encountered.

Factors to Consider

1. No teacher should have more than three periods in a row.

2. No teacher can have more than three different "preparations" (course codes).

3. Every teacher must have an official lunch period—4, 5, or 6.

4. Curricula vary by state. The Social Studies program here is just for practice.

5. The fifty-four Social Studies classes to be assigned are listed. They have been grouped by grade. Also note that courses are taught on three levels: Honors, Regular, Skills. Some multisection courses have *two* sections on the *same* period. Keep these in mind in dealing with requests for team teaching.

6. Twelfth grade classes are a bit tricky. There are two sections on each period. One teacher teaches Economics both semesters and one teaches Government both semesters; the students switch at midyear. Instead of a full-year course with one teacher, this configuration provides practice with teaming and half-year courses.

7. Special considerations for teachers with administrative/duty assignments are noted. Since these have been given in advance, they must be honored.

8. On the other hand, you don't have to honor teachers' requests. As a matter of fact, you *can't* honor them all. You will have to make some judgment calls.

9. Strive to give teachers balanced programs. Avoid giving one teacher five honors classes while giving another five lower level classes.

10. Room assignments will ultimately be made on the master plan, which follows.

11. The lines listed for the teachers are reserved for *class* assignments *only!* Don't be concerned at this point about anything else: duty assignments, preparation periods, lunch periods, professional periods, or any other nonteaching assignment(s).

12. Once your assignments are complete, transfer them to the grid. Some people don't like to use the lines; they prefer to go to the grid immediately.

13. Here is a good program: 10R–**4th,** 10R–**6th,** 11H–**1st,** 9S–**2nd,** 9S–**8th.** This teacher has three courses (9S, 10R, and 11H) and is teaching periods 1–2–4–6–8.

    Here is a poor program: 11R–**5th,** 11H–**7th,** 11H–**8th,** 10H–**1st,** 10R–**3rd.** It is unacceptable because there are four different courses (10R, 10H, 11R, 11H).

14. Nor is there just one right way to get started. There are several ways to go: Look at the "locks," those corner pieces. By putting them in (in red!), you already reduce your degree of choice. In other words, you started with fifty-four sections to assign; now the number has decreased, almost before you get started. *Or,* deal with the requests—if you deem them legitimate. *Or,* start with the singletons, then doubletons, and so on. *Or,* just go alphabetically, starting with "A" and working your work to the end.

Social Studies Classes to Assign to Teachers

Course	Number	Periods
SS 9 Honors	2	5, 7 (This means 5 *and* 7, *not* 5 through 7)
SS 9 Regular	10	1 1 2 2 3 4 5 6 7 8 (Two sections on some periods!)
SS 9 Skills	2	4, 8
SS 10 Honors	1	1
SS 10 Regular	10	1 2 3 4 5 6 7 7 8 8
SS 10 Skills	2	3 4
SS 11 Adv. Pl.	2	1 & 2 (This is one double-period class)
SS 11 Honors	1	2
SS 11 Regular	9	1 2 3 3 4 5 6 7 8
SS 11 Skills	1	7
SS 12 Humanities	2	3 & 4 (High-powered, one double-period class)
SS 12 Regular	8	1 1 2 2 6 6 7 7 (Remember teaming!)
SS 12 Skills	4	3 3 5 5 (12th grade teaming also for Skills)

Teacher Assignments

Now, let's meet our cast of characters—and study their requests.

Remember: The number of lines to write on = number of classes the teacher is assigned to teach.

Ames	Comes in early to call substitutes; 6th period = last teaching period. Only one schedule works: 1–2–3–5–6.	___	___	___	___	___
Bell	Union pres.; must be free 8th period. But also requesting free first period.	___	___	___	___	___
Crane	Leaving in two months; substitute unknown.	___	___	___	___	___
Davis	Requesting all Skills-level classes. Also asking for Grades 9 & 10.	___	___	___	___	___
Ellis	Requesting 11 AP course. Deputy chair; must be free the two periods chair (Fox) teaches.	___	___	___	___	
Fox	Department chair; must teach only periods 3 & 4—two sections of the same course.	___	___			

(Continued)

(Continued)

Gold	Advises student newspaper; requesting to be free 8th period. Also, would like only two different course preparations.	____ ____ ____ ____ ____
Harris	Wants to team teach with Ivy, any course—1 or 2 sections.	____ ____ ____ ____
Ivy	Wants to team teach with Harris, any course— 1 or 2 sections.	____ ____ ____ ____
Jones	Dean of Students; must teach periods 4, 5, and 7. Requesting 12th grade classes.	____ ____ ____
King	Business Education teacher, just became dual-certified in Social Studies. Assign two sections of same course periods 7 and 8.	____ ____
Lee	Runs the school store 6th period as a duty; still has five classes. Requesting 5th-period lunch and all 11th grade classes.	____ ____ ____ ____ ____
Masters	Part-time teacher from the Middle School; must teach periods 1–2–3.	____ ____ ____

USA High School—Social Studies Department Schedule—20__								
	1st	*2nd*	*3rd*	*4th*	*5th*	*6th*	*7th*	*8th*
Ames								
Bell								
Crane								
Davis								
Ellis .8								
Fox .4								
Gold								
Harris								
Ivy								
Jones .6								
King .4								
Lee								
Masters .6								

USA High School—Social Studies Department Room Master[7]								
Room No.	1st	2nd	3rd	4th	5th	6th	7th	8th
301								
302								
303								
304								
305								
306								
307								
308								
309								

The scheduling of rooms in Social Studies, as challenging as it may be, at least doesn't have the added complications science laboratories, computer facilities, shops, or special rooms usually do. With Social Studies, you're working with standard classrooms. Most other departments do have to be concerned about courses that require the use of special facilities. For example, if there are only four science labs, the schedulers must make sure that only four science lab courses are scheduled on any one period; if there are only three computer labs, buildingwide, the administrator overseeing the scheduling must make sure that only three courses—from all the different subject departments—requiring labs are scheduled for any one period.

Summary

All the preliminary steps have been accomplished. The curriculum has been planned and packaged, the information has been disseminated to parents and students, course requests have been tallied, potential conflicts have been identified and those troublemakers have been assigned to different periods, and the skeleton of the schedule has been constructed. Now it's time to begin the complex process of putting together all the other puzzle pieces and building the complete master schedule itself. This, understandably, was the longest chapter in the book. The complicated process was broken down into several more-manageable parts.

---

[7] I mentioned schools which have the luxury of giving each teacher her own room. In this case, the 13 Social Studies teachers are sharing 9 rooms. However, there are schools in which the room utilization is so tight that several departments share certain rooms—and the assignments must be done centrally by a building administrator, rather than the department head as in this case.

TASKS FOR STEP 6

In the introduction to this chapter, I listed the seven areas we would address. Let's break them down even farther into the specific tasks we described:

- *Setting up shop:* housekeeping concerns—where, when, and how the job is going to get done
- *Determining course loads for each teacher:* teacher assignment worksheet—once the number of sections for each department has been determined
- *Juggling all the variables:* thirty factors to consider when building the master schedule—not operating in isolation, but all impinging on one another
- *Deciding which of four building methods is best for your school:* size counts!—small, medium, and large schools
- *Understanding how delicate the schedule is:* an actual scenario—how moving even one section can produce a domino effect
- *Projecting the "building curve":* the correct number of sections per period—avoiding overcrowding and underutilization
- *Going beyond the mechanical:* personnel considerations—human factors to take into consideration in building the schedule
- *Putting it all together:* constructing the department schedule for a large Social Studies Department—with just about every possible complication

Step 7

Test It

Computer Simulation

Many master schedulers agree that Step 5 (Spot Trouble), the conflict matrix, is the most difficult step; Step 6 (Build It), constructing the actual schedule, is the most fun; but Step 7 (Test It), *computer simulation*, is the most fascinating.

Before simulation, once the schedule was completed, you had no clue as to how good it was. You didn't find out until students had been placed in sections. Thanks to computer simulation, the scheduler now gets a "report card" and a chance to make adjustments before the master is locked and students are loaded.

It's been a while since we looked at the student course requests. Now view them as being on a collision course: *What happens when those course requests go up against the master schedule just completed?*

What Is Simulation—and What Does It Tell Us?

Computer simulation pits the course requests against the final draft of the master schedule *before students are actually loaded* and lets you know how well your schedule works. Specifically, it gives you data in the following categories. Note that software packages vary as to what reports they generate; these are the most common:

1. Percentage of Students Successfully Scheduled. This is the number one barometer. What percentage of students received successful schedules—with the courses they wanted . . . in sections the correct size . . . with no conflicts . . . and no gaps.

2. Conflicts. We never said that we could eliminate all conflicts. The purpose of the conflict matrix in Step 5 was to *minimize* the number. Now, it will become evident as to which students ended up with unresolved conflicts.

3. Closed Classes. You may find that some students have workable schedules, getting all of the classes they want, but they end up in oversized classes. This tells you that there may not be enough sections on certain periods.

4. Invalid Codes. Go back to Step 2; now you will see why a logical system of course codes is so critical. Invariably there will be students who are "rejected" because they have course codes that don't exist. With thousands of entries, clerical mistakes are inevitable; keep them to a minimum. If not corrected earlier, they surface now.

5. Canceled Classes. In Step 4, while we attempted to reconcile teacher supply and teacher demand, there was considerable discussion as to which courses would run and which would be canceled. Were counselors notified of these decisions so that course requests could be adjusted, removing canceled classes and substituting alternates? Canceled classes, still on student schedules, will turn up in Step 7.

6. Overscheduled. It's the nine-pound baloney in the eight-pound bag. Some students may have ended up with more courses than they can possibly fit into their schedules. This problem is particularly acute in schools with many half-year courses. Remember: Two half-year courses must be counted as a single full-year course.

7. Underscheduled. Similarly, after adding and dropping requests, some schedules may end up short, with gaps. If that's not permissible, it can be corrected in several ways: first, by adding a study hall; second, by consolidating the schedule and permitting early dismissal; third, by inserting additional subjects. If students must have full schedules, then it is imperative at this point to identify those who have gaps.

Simulation Statistics

Take a look at this format for presenting simulation statistics. Keep in mind that each software package has its own way of presenting these same data:

Grade	Acceptable	Rejected	Percentage
9	435	65	87
10	470	30	94
11	410	90	82
12	365	135	73
Totals/Average	**1,680**	**320**	**84**

Look at the last column; two things are evident. First, the percentage of students with acceptable schedules decreases from the ninth to the twelfth grade. No surprise; freshmen tend to take more multisection bread 'n' butter courses and relatively few electives. As a result, it's easier to work out acceptable schedules for them. Advancing to the sophomore, junior, and senior years, students tend to take more electives and singletons. Their schedules are more prone to conflicts, thereby lowering the percentage of acceptable schedules. By senior year, the percentage drops to 73 percent (I have seen first-run simulation percentages below 50%). We'll provide three remedies.

First, though, let's look at a number that is *not* expected. Why is the percentage for freshmen so low? One guidance counselor had inadvertently used the wrong lunch code for her ninth grade counselees. Consequently, all of those students "kicked out," thereby drastically reducing the number of acceptable schedules. Once this error was easily corrected, the percentage for freshmen rose to almost 100 percent in the next run.

Here's the point: Without simulation, the scheduler would never have known about this easy-to-correct error until opening day when all those freshmen would be incorrectly scheduled. See the value of simulation? We've only just begun.

Objective of Simulation

The purpose of simulation, then, is to do a run . . . ascertain the percentage . . . make changes . . . and do another run, hopefully improving the percentage each time. This process can be repeated again and again and again until all the students have acceptable schedules before the master is locked and the students are actually loaded into the sections. Try, try, and try again until you approach 100 percent.

Some errors are relatively easy to clean up. Look for students with invalid codes, canceled courses, too many subjects, too few subjects, duplicate course codes (accidentally listed twice), and so on. Fixing just these errors will "up" your percentage significantly. Do another run to find out. But then come the more complicated problems requiring more challenging solutions. There are three strategies—move students, move sections, and change priority numbers:

1. Move Students. If you ascertain that a student has an irresolvable conflict, she may be forced to make a choice. Look at an alternate already designated. If there is no alternate, send for the student, inform her of the problem, and let her decide between the two (or more) courses in conflict. A word of caution, however. If you see a trend where the same course seems to be popping up as a troublemaker, consider doing something about the *course*, rather than the student. More about that possibility below.

> **√ Helpful Hint 35**
>
> Some computer software packages provide a summary of courses that posed problems during the scheduling simulation. If yours doesn't, just keep a running list of your own. For example, if you see that Music Theory keeps turning up as a problem, you may want to look at the way the course is scheduled.

If the student is going to be forced to make a choice because of an irresolvable conflict, you will need to notify her. Having that list of alternative choices will prove helpful at this point, but you still may have to get in touch with her.

> **√ Helpful Hint 36**
>
> Back in Step 2, a list was made of those courses on the cusp of being canceled. A similar list was also maintained for courses for which you needed to recruit students. Go to these lists now. Doing this will serve two purposes: First, it will give students suggestions as to alternates they can take if faced with irresolvable conflicts; second, this is a splendid opportunity to build up those classes with students who now need courses.

√ **Helpful Hint 37**

Below is a sample form that you can easily adapt for notifying students that they have a conflict and must make a decision between two (or more) courses:

Conflict Notification Form

Student _____ Counselor_____

Dear Student:

   We have run your course requests through the computer and have determined that you have one or more conflicts:

_____ and _____
_____ and _____

   A conflict means that you have requested two courses that cannot be accommodated in your schedule, probably because they are both being offered during the same period. Therefore, you must make a choice: Pick one or the other. Please *circle* the course you would like to keep and put a *line* through the one you wish to drop.

   At this time, you may select another course (if it is still open and it fits into your schedule) to take the place of the course you are dropping. Listed below are several suggestions:

_____, _____, _____

   Since we want you to understand and be a part of what's happening throughout every step of the scheduling process, your counselor will be happy to discuss this decision with you and answer any questions you have. Please return this form to your counselor *no later than* _____.

   Thank you for your cooperation.
   Signature of administrator in charge of scheduling

Sometimes, however, when you meet with students, their decisions will surprise you. Take a look at these data from "the reject listing," a report coming from the simulation. This format is the easiest to read because the work has been done for you.

Conflicts by Student			
Smith, John	English 12 General (7th)	*and*	Carpentry (7th)

   When John meets with his counselor to resolve the conflict, the expectation is that he will switch to another elective. John, however, explains that he has his heart set on Carpentry. To the counselor's surprise, he would like to switch the English 12 General. The counselor explains that the only alternative is regular English 12. John said that he'd rather take that than give up Carpentry. After a discussion as to the feasibility of this decision, as well as consultation with the department head, it is decided that he should be able to handle the regular class. The counselor is glad that he met with John. Otherwise, he would have *assumed* that John would have taken another elective. Of course, this is an oversimplification, but it makes the point. Unfortunately, many conflict resolutions don't work out so easily; hard choices are more often the rule.

- In some scheduling software packages, the computer shows you the schedule *minus* the courses in conflict—and you have to figure out what the problem is.
- In others, the computer makes the decision for you. For example, in John's case above, it might have scheduled the English 12 General since it is a core course, and "kicked out" the elective.
- In still others, more sophisticated, an actual scheduling grid is printed out so that you can pinpoint the conflict. All sections for all courses originally requested are listed.
- On occasion, you may come up against students with two, three, or more conflicts. As one student sadly bemoaned, "Everything I want seems to be fourth period." She happened to be right. Even with students taking entirely different course combinations, there will be those unfortunate ones who will have to make several hard choices.

Look at this rejected schedule. The courses the student is taking are listed—as well as the periods when they are offered. The period that is suggested for each course has been bolded.

Code	Course Title	Periods	Message
103	English 11 Honors	1–3–4–6–7	******conflict*****
203	Social Studies 11 AP	**1**	
303	Math 11 Honors	1–**3**	
403	Chemistry Honors	1–3–**5**	
503	Spanish 3	3–4–6–**7**	
800	Orchestra	**6**	
901	Health/Physical Education (alt.)	1–2–3–4–5–6–7–**8**	
001	Lunch	**4**–5–6	

Follow the logic of the computer as it attempts to schedule this.

Orchestra is a singleton, so it is locked in *sixth* period.

Social Studies 11 Advanced Placement (AP) is also a singleton; it can go only *first* period.

Math 11 Honors is a doubleton (1–3), but you've already used period 1, so you have to schedule it on *third*.

Chemistry Honors is offered three periods (1–3–5), but you've already used two of them. Therefore, this course is put on *fifth* period. Remember, we're treating science classes as single periods, without labs, which could further complicate matters.

Better schedule lunch. Only *fourth* period lunch is left.

Spanish 3 is offered four different periods (3–4–6–7); unfortunately, we've used three of them. There is no choice but to schedule it for *seventh* period.

English 11 Honors is offered five different periods. By this time we've already used all of them. The computer scheduled the other courses earlier because there were fewer sections. Now English is "odd man out." The remaining course, Health/Physical Education, meets every period, but that doesn't help English. Look closely: The problem is that *nothing* this student wants is *second* period. Yes, you could put Health/Physical Education on *second* period—but then there would be nothing for *eighth* period.

There are at least three possible solutions to this problem:

- One of the courses scheduled earlier could be changed to an alternate to open up a needed period to accommodate English.
- The student might have to take English 11 Regular as an alternate.
- In extreme cases, the student might give up a lunch period to accommodate all the classes she wants. This is a common problem with Honors students who take so many singletons.

Reserve these for those on the team who like logic puzzles such as Sudoku.

2. Move Sections. Sometimes it's not the students, but the sections that have to be moved. For example, a section on a particular period just isn't loading well. Let's take a look at two examples:

Crafts: (requests: 95)

Section	Period	Load	Maximum
01	3	25	25
02	5	22	25
03	6	11	25
04	8	23	25

A total of eighty-one students loaded into these four sections out of ninety-five original requests; the computer was unable to schedule fourteen students. Yet, there is plenty of room sixth period. For some reason, it didn't load well. Maybe the students taking this course were taking *other* courses that used sixth period before Crafts was scheduled. Whatever the case, a change is in order. Move the class off sixth and try a different period, but which one? You could go by trial and error, or review the "reject listing" of several students who didn't get this course scheduled and determine which period(s) work for them. Suppose that of the first three students you check, two could take it seventh period. Give it a shot: Move section 3 from period 6 to period 7.

Another curious fact about these figures: The maximum (or "cap") is twenty-five. Look at third period. Every one of the twenty-five seats is taken. Suppose there was no cap or there was a *second* section of this course on third period. Would those other fourteen students have been successfully scheduled? More on using the cap below. Now, a second example:

English 12 Advanced Placement (requests: 39)

Section	Period	Load	Maximum
01	4	13	25
02	7	13	25

Note that only twenty-six of the thirty-nine requests were met. One third of the students were not able to get this course into their schedules—unacceptable for such a high-powered class, but not surprising given the number of singletons seniors tend to take. Take advantage of the fact that simulations can be done in a matter of minutes (or seconds). Through trial and error, try every possible combination of periods until you find two that accommodate most students: 4 and 8, 3 and 7, 3 and 4, and so on. Let's hope you hit the right combination, but if you don't, there is one last chance.

3. Change Priority Numbers. Students have been moved, sections have been moved, yet there still are a few bad pennies, courses that, no matter what you try, don't load well. You have one more option: change priority numbers. I call it, "Cut the line." Use this method very sparingly.

Remember: The computer schedules courses based on the number of sections offered, from least to most. In the above example, the singletons are "locked" first; there's no choice. If there is more than one singleton, most computers will place the core subject first. Suppose, for example, that the student had signed up for two classes that were both singletons. English 10 Remedial happened to be *eighth only* . . . and Keyboarding happened to be *second only.* No problem. Suppose, however, that both singletons happen to be *eighth only.* There is a conflict already. English will probably be scheduled first. Keyboarding is out of luck; the student will have to take another elective. But suppose you wanted every student to take Keyboarding. You could program the computer to schedule Keyboarding ahead of English, "cutting the line," and forcing the student to have to take an alternate to English 10 Remedial. Simply put, the priority number is the order in which courses are scheduled. You can manually tamper with that number to give certain courses an advantage.

In the example above in which we looked at the reject listing, the singletons were scheduled first, followed by the doubleton, followed by the tripleton, followed by the course with five sections. The last course to be scheduled, obviously, was the alternating-day Health/Physical Education because it was offered every period. By the time the computer reached it, most (if not all) other periods were used up. But there is another issue to face: Is there *room?* Maybe all of the seats have been taken in the specific section the student needs by the time she is reached. More on "closed classes" ahead. For now: As the number of sections increases . . . the degree of choice decreases.

Now, let's return to that conundrum with English 12 Advanced Placement. No matter what we tried, nothing seemed to work. Again, this was due in large measure to the fact that this advanced student is taking many other high-powered courses, most of them probably singletons. No combination of periods seemed to work. What scheduling strategy is left? Change the priority number for English 12 Advanced Placement, or, "cut the line"! This course is a doubleton; singletons are being scheduled before it.

√ Helpful Hint 38

Most scheduling software packages allow you to manually instruct the computer to let a particular course—here, English 12 AP—go first, with other classes scheduled after it. You are now assured that English 12 AP is scheduled. But there are dangers with this approach. By letting it slip in, you may have increased the number of conflicts with courses that were bumped.

To repeat: Changing priority numbers should be done sparingly. If you "cut the line" for many courses, you'll be right back where you started from. Still, it is a valuable tool if you want to guarantee that a course gets scheduled early in the game.

Before we go on to the final section in this chapter, let's look at some of the other valuable information that simulation data can yield. Take a look at the following report:

Code	Course	Section	Period	Teacher	Assigned	Maximum
(74 out of 74 students loaded: 100%)						
101	English 9G	01	02	Black	18	20
101	English 9G	02	03	Green	19	20
101	English 9G	03	05	Grey	19	20
101	English 9G	04	08	White	18	20
(354 out of 372 students loaded: 95%)						
102	English 9R	01	01	Green	26	30
102	English 9R	02	01	Brown	27	30
102	English 9R	03	02	Black	16	30
102	English 9R	04	02	White	15	30
102	English 9R	05	03	Black	30	30
102	English 9R	06	04	Green	28	30
102	English 9R	07	04	White	28	30
102	English 9R	08	05	Black	29	30
102	English 9R	09	06	Grey	30	30
102	English 9R	10	07	Brown	19	20
102	English 9R	11	07	White	30	30
102	English 9R	12	08	Grey	26	30
102	English 9R	13	08	Black	25	30
102	English 9R	14	08	Green	25	30
(74 out of 76 students loaded: 97%)						
103	English 9H	01	04	Black	30	30
103	English 9H	02	06	White	27	30
103	English 9H	03	07	Grey	17	30

We can learn a great deal from this report. Let's study it course by course.

- There are four sections of English 9G with four different teachers. The sections couldn't have loaded better: With a cap of twenty, the sections are eighteen—nineteen—nineteen—eighteen. In other words, the computer divided the seventy-four students equally among the four sections.
- At the opposite end, the three sections of English 9 Honors are not terrible—but not great, either: thirty—twenty-seven—seventeen. That section with seventeen is troubling. It is respectable in size, but note the considerable imbalance among the three sections. Try moving it to another period in simulation, but be prepared to get even worse results. You may find that that imbalance is the best you can do. On the other hand, every single seat is used in the

fourth period class. In addition, two students didn't load at all. If the cap were thirty-two, would they have been scheduled into that section? Temporarily raise the cap to see what happens. Depending on your district's policies, you very well might have to lower it back to thirty, but at least you will learn some valuable information about where sections are needed.

√ Helpful Hint 39

Maybe you can increase the maximum . . . maybe you can't. But here's a trick that may prove helpful. Look at *other* subjects that these students are taking. Perhaps if you open a section of a *different* course on this period, that section will absorb some of these students. Look at the schedule in other departments. As a matter of fact, you may discover a similar problem with a class (or classes) on the same period. The schedule is telling you that you need an additional section on that particular period. Let's take this hint to another level. Suppose you discover that Social Studies 10 sections are packed on fifth period. You have two of them. Try as you might, there is no possible way to move another section to fifth period for a third section. *It doesn't have to be a Social Studies class.* Look back at the other core courses with multiple sections: Try moving an English 10, Math 10, or Science 10 section to the fifth period to absorb students searching for a class that period in their schedule.

- Finally, look at the fourteen sections of English 9R: "Unsatisfactory." To begin with, eighteen students didn't get scheduled, and that's perplexing, especially since you have at least one section on every period. Let's go period by period:
  - Period 1 is fine: two sections, one with twenty-six and one with twenty-seven.
  - You have two sections on period 2, but you probably don't need them. The computer had trouble finding students to put in two. It took thirty-one students and divided them in half (16 + 15). Keep one of these sections in your pocket in case you need it.
  - On first glance, period 3 looks good. Every seat is taken (30). But the question is, if the cap had been higher or if there had been a second section, would more students have been absorbed on this period? The only way to find out is to do an additional run. Perhaps you can convert that unneeded second period section into a third period class, at least temporarily.
  - Fourth period is just about perfect, with fifty-six students divided up over two sections. There is still room for four more students. Don't touch it.
  - Fifth period is fine with just one section.
  - Sixth period poses the same question as we had with third period. All thirty seats are taken in this single section. Is this one enough, or could you use a second? You can't tell because of the "thirty" maximum.
  - Seventh period appears to be fine. Note the smaller cap on Section 10. This is a Special Education inclusion class with a lower register. Two sections appear to be adequate, although it is a bit tight with room for only one more student between them.
  - There are three sections on period 8; the scheduler projected the need correctly. All three not only filled nicely, but all three are close to capacity.

Hence, this loading report was chock-full of information for the scheduler, especially when it was checked period by period. Additional simulation runs are worthwhile for checking section placement and trying to smooth out imbalances.

To Cap or Not to Cap

In the previous section, I alluded to information that can be obtained from lifting, at least temporarily, the cap on certain sections. The final section of this chapter is devoted to lifting the caps completely during the early computer runs.

I stated above that Health and Physical Education was the last course to be scheduled because it had the most sections, with one offered on every period. However, we did not take into consideration whether there was room in all those sections. Suppose that we are talking about "PE 10," which all 240 sophomores take. Ideally, those eight sections for those eight periods will load like this:

	1	2	3	4	5	6	7	8
PE 10	30	30	30	30	30	30	30	30

Wouldn't that be nice. It would mean that things worked out perfectly and you had created precisely the correct number of sections per period. Suppose, however, that the course loaded something like this:

	1	2	3	4	5	6	7	8
PE 10	20	30	30	16	30	25	23	9

Now you've got your work cut out for you. To begin with, fifty-seven students didn't load at all. Would they have been successfully scheduled had there been more room in periods 2, 3, and/or 5? We don't know—but we can find out. Similarly, note the poor loading on period 4 and especially on period 8. We wanted a section on every period, but perhaps across all departments, there are too many fourth and eighth period classes. By the time the computer schedules PE 10, it can't find enough students to fill those periods.

> **√ Helpful Hint 40**
>
> For the early scheduling simulation runs, temporarily lift the cap to let the computer place the students where it needs to. This will provide you with invaluable information.

Let's take this concept one step farther. Suppose, for example, that Social Studies 10R is the very last course the computer loads in because it is the course with the most sections. And suppose you decide *not* to cap during the early runs, letting the computer place students where the course will fit into their schedule. What valuable information would you learn? Look at the following loading report for Social Studies 10R:

Section	Period	Teacher	Assigned	Maximum[1]
01	01	Carpenter	25	100
02	01	Taylor	24	100
03	02	Carpenter	15	100
04	02	Miner	15	100
05	02	Cook	15	100
06	03	Gardener	17	100
07	04	Carpenter	24	100
08	04	Miner	24	100
09	04	Cook	23	100
10	05	Miner	24	100
11	05	Gardener	24	100
12	06	Carpenter	27	100
13	07	Cook	20	100
14	08	Gardener	42	100
15	08	Cook	41	100

What can we learn from this loading report? Again, let's go period by period.

- It's an auspicious start: There are two sections on period 1 and both loaded perfectly, with twenty-five and twenty-four.
- Period 2 is another story. There are three sections, with fifteen students in each section. At the end of the line, the computer could find only forty-five students for the second period 10R classes and then divided them equally among the three sections. We don't need three sections; two will accommodate the forty-five students, with one section of twenty-three and one of twenty-two. Therefore, we can abolish one section and save it in case we need it later.
- There is only one section on period 3 and it loaded with seventeen. Light, but we'll keep it to have a section every period. Also, it will grow with transfers and new admits.
- We're back to three sections for period 4. But this time all three loaded nicely with twenty-four, twenty-four, and twenty-three students. Three sections was a good call here.
- Ditto for period 5. There are two sections, the correct number, with twenty-four in both.
- There are twenty-seven students in the sole section on period 6. Large, but not large enough to justify another section. Mark it "closed"; no additional students will go into this class.

---

[1] There are two ways to lift the cap. Some programs ask you point blank whether you want to observe the maximum class size during the runs. All you have to do is say "No" during the initial runs. In others, all you have to do is set the cap at some inflated number, in this case 100.

- Period 7, on the other hand, is a bit light with twenty. But once again, this is the only section on this period, so we'll keep it and build it up, if possible.
- Period 8 is the most revealing. There are two sections. Remember: We didn't cap at twenty-five. As a result, eighty-three students were divided between the two sections, one with forty-two and one with forty-one. Obviously, we need a third section here. Those eighty-three students will then be in sections of twenty-eight, twenty-eight, and twenty-seven. A bit large, but certainly manageable for now. *We would not have known the need for this third section if we had capped at thirty!* By not capping for this run, we let the chips fall where they would. In other words, eighty-three students needed an eighth period class at the end of the scheduling process.

But where does this additional section come from? Think back to period 2, when we had a third section we didn't need. We put it in our pocket. Now, it's time to take it out and use it. One of the second period classes will be abolished . . . and an additional eighth period class will be created. The numbers work, but what about the department schedule? Let's take a look at the fifteen 10R sections as well as the other classes:

	1	2	3	4	5	6	7	8
Carpenter	10R	10R		10R		10R		10H
Cook		10R	10H	10R			10R	10R
Gardener	9R	9R	10R		10R			10R
Miner	9R	10R		10R	10R		9R	(10R)
Taylor (.2)	10R							

Can any of the 10R teachers scheduled to teach second period move to eighth? Miner can; the schedule shows her to be unassigned eighth period, so a switch is possible. After consulting the department head, a move will be made on Miner's schedule *from* period 2 *to* period 8. Of course, things don't always work out this easily. Suppose that none of the three second period teachers was available eighth period. There are three other options.

- First, other 10R teachers who are not teaching second period can be brought into the mix, with more sections being shuffled until there is one fewer on period 2.
- Second, if none of the 10R teachers is available, a more extensive shuffle involving other teachers in the department not teaching 10R might be necessary.
- Third, as mentioned before, if none of the teachers' schedules is subject to change, we can look to another department. The problem: How to absorb more tenth graders on the eighth period? It doesn't have to be Social Studies. We can look at English, Math, Science, Foreign Language, or even a predominantly tenth grade elective (as indicated by the original tally). An additional eighth period class in one of those other departments will cut the demand down for the third section in Social Studies.

The loading for Social Studies 10R is now satisfactory. This was possible because we decided to lift the cap, temporarily, to gain valuable scheduling information.

Summary

Almost every scheduling software package offers simulation, although both the specific reports as well as their formats vary greatly. We focused on the simulation reports that shed light on the master schedule and dramatically increase the percentage of students who can be successfully scheduled without conflicts and in sections that have room. Simulation tells you if you have the sections on right periods, both in terms of accommodating student requests and balancing class sizes. For now, you need to be most concerned with reports that can be used as tools to increase the percentage of students successfully scheduled. If your district is in the market for a software package, the master scheduler needs to be involved in the search as well as in the ultimate selection process. The quality of simulation reports is an important criterion, so consider that before making the purchase.

TASKS FOR STEP 7

Scheduling simulation provides critical information for adjusting the master schedule prior to loading students into sections. The scheduler must become familiar with all of the reports that can be generated with regard to schedules, conflicts, rooms, periods, and the like. These reports yield data used to clean things up prior to Step 8.

Step 8

Load It

*Three Methods for Loading
Students Into the Schedule*

There is no end to the number of simulation runs you can do. But eventually, it becomes counterproductive: one step forward, two steps back. In scheduling terms, you remedy one conflict situation . . . but create another. It's time to let go. When you're satisfied that the master schedule is the best it can possibly be, "lock" it. I use the word *lock* because that's precisely what you're doing. The results can be disastrous if you don't. You print schedules . . . make some minor changes. To your dismay, when you do another run, they've been shuffled and you get an altogether different result.

There is a variety of terms for schedule changes *after* the master has been locked. My favorite is *maintenance*. That word says it all. The infrastructure is in stone; view any changes to student or teacher schedules as repairs.[1]

So, at last, the final simulation has been run . . . tinkering with the sections is now over . . . and you're satisfied with the master. Lock it. To repeat: This is not to say that changes are over; probably far from it. But the master schedule is in stone and any changes will have to be done manually and individually.

---

[1] Consider what would happen if you created a new section of a course. *Before* maintenance, on the next run—that additional section would load, just like all the others. Suppose you went from four to five sections of English 11. Before maintenance, on this run, the computer would divide the students among five, rather than four sections. It's an entirely different story *after* the schedule has been locked and when you're on maintenance. The only changes on subsequent runs will be the individual ones made by counselors. That fifth section of English 11 will have no students in it—*unless* the counselors manually assign them.

> **√ Helpful Hint 41**
>
> Locking the schedule and moving to maintenance should be done with some ceremony—and for good reason. Make sure that anyone and everyone connected with scheduling (assistant principals, interns, guidance counselors, members of the scheduling team) are aware when you turn the key. Major problems are on the horizon if the move to maintenance comes unbeknownst to those who access the schedule.[2]

Loading Students

There are three methods for loading students into the sections of the master schedule. The size of your school will be a major factor in determining which method you use: by computer, by hand, or by arena. Today, most large schools rely on the computer to do the job, while many smaller schools prefer to schedule manually. More about the third option, arena scheduling, later in the chapter. The advantages and disadvantages of each will be discussed. Although the three are very different, they share a common thread, one that was explained in Step 7: *The greater the number of sections . . . the later the course is scheduled in the process; the fewer the number of sections . . . the earlier the course is scheduled in the process.* It's common sense.

Recall what has been said repeatedly regarding "the givens." It applies to all three loading methods. Look at the courses the student is taking: Lock in the singletons, then schedule the doubletons, then move to the tripletons, then to the courses that have four sections, and so forth. End up with the courses that have the most sections. Some may meet every period of the day. In large schools, there may be many multisection courses. The logic is clear: By the time you reach these multisection courses, many periods have been used up. On the other hand, these courses have the most options. Hopefully, at least one period that is needed will be available at the end of the line.

Take a look at the courses Mary is taking—as well as the periods they are offered. Her schedule works only one way. Which course would be scheduled first? Second? Last? The selected periods are in bold. Reconstruct how this schedule was put together. Use the list of periods on the right to do the scheduling; cross off the period when you use it. This is a very important exercise:

Courses	Periods Available	
English 11	1–**3**–4–5–6–7	~~1~~
Social Studies 11H	4–5–**6**	~~2~~
Math 11	**2**–4–5–7	~~3~~

(Continued)

---

[2] I recall a situation in which the scheduler forgot to "lock" the schedule and move to maintenance. Everyone was reasonably happy with the schedule. Counselors did some fine-tuning to their counselees' schedules. A new run of schedules reflecting those adjustments was ordered. To his dismay, the computer totally shuffled the students' schedules—new sections, new periods—because he had forgotten to lock the master. It was back to square one, insofar as having students review their schedules was concerned. All that time and work had been wasted.

(Continued)

Courses	Periods Available	
Oceanography/Marine Bio	4–5	**4**
Spanish 3	1–4–5–6–7	**5**
Chorus	5	**6**
Physical Education/Health	1–2–3–4–5–6–7–8	**7**
Lunch	4–5–6–7	**8**

The subjects are scheduled in the following order: Chorus . . . Oceanography/ Marine Biology . . . Social Studies 11H . . . Lunch . . . Spanish 3 . . . Math 11 . . . English 11 . . . Physical Education/ Health. Make sure you understand why. The value of having two half-year courses line up so nicely becomes apparent from this example.

There is only one way that Mary's schedule works, but there is one other factor that could prevent her from getting this schedule: There has to be room in the sections she needs among the multisection courses. Suppose that by the time English 11 is reached, the third period section is full. That could pose a problem. Now you understand the extreme importance of placing the correct number of sections per period. In theory, the computer has the power to place the students where they need a particular course. Put another way, another student won't get the section Mary needs, if that other student can be placed in a different section on a different period.

√ Helpful Hint 42

By this point in the process, you will notice that piles and piles of reports are stacking up. After seven scheduling steps, going all the way back to the course catalogue and the original tallies, there's quite an inventory. Do not throw *any* of these out until *after* the current scheduling season is over. Invariably you are going to have to look back at some decisions you made earlier; if you throw away the evidence, you may be sorry. Instead, get an empty paper carton. Put it in an out-of-the-way corner. Toss all the old documents in the box, keeping them in reverse chronological order with the most recent document on top. You never know when you may need to refer to them. Once the scheduling cycle is over, it's OK to discard or shred everything.

Method 1—By Computer: Most computer programs will ask you a series of questions before loading students into the schedule. Here are some of the variables:

- How many tries/seconds should the computer spend on each schedule?
- In what order should the computer schedule students? By grade? Alphabetically? Complexity? (Level of difficulty?)
- Should caps (maximum class size) be strictly adhered to?
- Should sections be balanced? By sex? By grade? By feeder school?
- Do you want to include personal information? You may want to omit the personal information, at least for now, given the strict rules under the new privacy laws.

A schedule will ultimately be printed for every student. In addition, several reports will be issued. One is a loading report, listing every section by course and the number of students assigned. Study this document carefully for irregularities in class size. The second document is yet another reject listing. Despite your best efforts, there still may be some students who have conflicts or who are closed out of sections they need. Work together with the counseling staff to adjust these schedules.

√ Helpful Hint 43

From now on, you're going to receive a sections list (i.e., loading report) on a regular basis. I call it my "tickertape." It doesn't have changing stock prices, but it does have something even more important, at least for the scheduler: updated section sizes. Before school opens as well as during the first few weeks of classes, this document should be updated every day. During peak scheduling times—maybe twice a day.

- The date of the report should be written in red in the upper right-hand corner.
- Each day's report should be printed on a different color paper.
- These documents should be filed in chronological order for ready reference.
- The most current report should have a prominent place on your desk.
- Copies should be distributed to everyone on the scheduling team.

√ Helpful Hint 44

Put on another pot of coffee, buy some donuts, and assemble your counselors and administrators around the table. Run a set of student schedules and divide them among those assembled. Have them go through the schedules in their pile to make sure (1) there are no conflicts, (2) students are not overscheduled (too many subjects), and (3) students are not underscheduled (too few subjects) leaving gaps in the day. You can add any other criteria to this list, which is unique to your school. By the time you're done, you have a complete run of "perfect" schedules ready to send home with students.

It's almost the end of the school year. You're ready to mail schedules home. Some administrators send them *without* teachers' names. It's a case of "trauma now versus trauma later." Why withhold this information? Of course, if your master is in flux, teacher assignments are in question, or you still have several vacancies, those are valid reasons *not* to print teacher names at this point. Otherwise, be up front. Deal with any issues now rather than later.

√ Helpful Hint 45

I am sure my colleagues would agree that requests for teacher changes trump the list of parent requests. This is the bane of administrators. Schools need a strict policy regarding teacher requests and teacher changes. Use your cabinet and/or scheduling committee to develop a *firm* policy. Some schools have a provision whereby students don't have to repeat with a teacher with whom they failed—where possible. (In smaller schools, this may be difficult to avoid.) This issue needs to be discussed until consensus is reached. I can't stress enough the need to publish your policy and adhere to it. There can be no exceptions. Need I tell you what will happen the first time you cave?

At last—the schedules are done. Send them home with a letter similar to this one.

√ Helpful Hint 46

Dear Student/Parent:

Attached is your schedule for the next school year.

Remember what we have been saying all along about the course selection process being a "contract"? Do you remember the chicken–fish–roast beef story? Teachers are hired and assigned and classes are formed based on the course requests you made. We expect you to stick to those commitments.

Review your schedule *carefully*. Make sure that you have all the *courses* you requested on the correct *levels*. You may find a different elective from the one you originally requested. This change could have occurred for one of two reasons: The original class was canceled because of low enrollment, or the course didn't fit into your schedule and we needed to use an alternate. If there is an error, fill out the form below and return it to your counselor by _____. *Please* do *not* call the office at this time.

Under **no circumstances** will the following requests be considered:

- Teacher changes
- Course changes
- Lunch period changes

Of course, your schedule is based on your passing all of your present courses. So do your very best as we come down the home stretch. Again: Review your schedule. If it is correct, there is nothing you need to do. If, however, you find one of the errors referred to above, fill out the form below and return it to the Counseling Office. We want to make these changes now so that the school will open on the first day with everyone in the correct place and "business as usual." Thank you for your cooperation.

_____
Signature of Administrator

_____

Dear Counselor:

I have reviewed my schedule for next year and I noted the following error(s), which should be corrected. (**Remember**: no course, teacher, or lunch period changes!)

_____

_____

_____

_____

_____

_____

(Please print! Please describe in detail. Return this form to the Counseling Office.)

Name_____

Counselor_____

Method 2—By Hand: Your school may decide to schedule the students by hand for one of two reasons: There is no computer to do the job or the school is small enough so that hand scheduling is feasible. In addition, summer schools, alternative schools, and many middle schools prefer to do the job by hand. But even if you rely on a computer, it is wise to be at least familiar with how this is done manually. Basically, the process is the same as with computer scheduling: Start with the singletons . . . move to the doubletons . . . tripletons . . . and continue to the multisection courses:

Column 1	Column 2	Column 3
Subjects **John is taking**	**Excerpts** **of the schedule**	**Periods** **available**
English 9 ___	1–3–4–5–6–7–8 ___	1
Social Studies 9 H ___	4 and 7 ___	2
Math 1 ___	3–4–5–7 ___	3
Biology ___	1–3–5–6–7 ___	4
French 2 ___	7 ___	5
Crafts ___	6 ___	6
Physical Education ___	1–2–3–4–5–6–7–8 ___	7
Lunch ___	5–6–7 ___	8

Study the sample scheduling card above. Column 1 lists John's courses; column 2 lists excerpts from the master schedule, the periods when those courses are offered; column 3 lists the open periods. Think of it as a Sudoku puzzle. Let's see how it works.

- As you know, we'll lock the singletons in first because they have no leeway. Look at column 2; there are two singletons, French 2 and Crafts. Which should you lock in first? Probably the French, because it is a core or required course, while Crafts is an elective. But since they are on two different periods, there is no problem. Put a check mark next to the period for those courses in column 2 . . . enter a "7" next to French 2 and a "6" next to Crafts in column 1. Now, go to column 3 and cross out the 7 and 6. In other words, you have already used the seventh and sixth periods; you can't use them again. Three steps: It's that simple!
- What's the next class to schedule? Social Studies 9 Honors is a doubleton, meeting on periods 4 and 7. Which one should you use? You have no choice; you've already used period 7 for French 2, so you'll have to use period 4 for this class. Repeat the procedure: Put a check mark next to the period in column 2; enter the "4" next to Social Studies 9 Honors in column 1; cross off the 4 in column 3.
- Let's go to the tripleton, lunch. We'd better schedule it now. Periods 6 and 7 are already used, so you have no choice except period 5. Place the check mark . . . enter the "5" in column 1 . . . cross off the 5 in column 3.
- Next up is Math 1. The good news is that it is offered on four periods; the bad news is that you've already used three of them. Again, you have no choice: Place the check mark . . . enter a "3" on the line in column 1 . . . cross off the 3 in the third column.

- There are five sections of Biology—but there is only one available period: 1. Follow the three steps: Place the check mark . . . enter the "1" in column 1 . . . and cross off the 1 in column 3.
- Just two courses to go, but we're running out of periods. English 9 comes next because it has the least number of sections of the two remaining courses. There are six sections on six different periods, but you've already used five of them. Fortunately, period 8 is still available. Do the drill: Place the check mark . . . enter an "8" in the first column . . . and cross out the 8 in the last column. (We're assuming there is room left in that section.)
- Now you're left with one course: Physical Education, which is offered every period. You have no choice, however; you've used every period except one. The only period available is 2. Finish the scheduling by placing the check mark . . . entering the "2" in column 1 . . . and crossing off the 2 in column 3.

John has been successfully scheduled. Of course, this example was contrived to show you the procedure as well as the logic behind it. The same methodical steps would be followed for all students. This is precisely how the computer does it.

You can adapt this model to hand scheduling your students. It is very useful for small high schools, alternative schools, summer schools, and middle schools. Here are the specific steps you would need to follow to develop a hand scheduling system. Note the tremendous attention to detail. If you go this route, you will need a highly organized person to implement this plan. Not interested in hand scheduling? Skip this section.

Step 1: Prepare a separate scheduling card for each student. Invest in heavier card stock. Color code the cards, with different colors for boys versus girls, special populations (such as English as a Second Language, Special Education, etc.), or to identify students coming from different feeder schools. If you are scheduling ninth graders coming from four different middle schools, use four different colors (blue, pink, yellow, and green) to identify them by school. In this way, you can create a good mix from the four schools in each section.

Step 2: In the first column, list the courses the student is taking, as in the example above. Or, you may wish to preprint all the courses offered and circle the ones that the particular student is taking. The card might look something like this:

English 9 Honors

⟨English 9 Regular⟩

English 9 Remedial

Step 3: Develop a list of *scheduling* codes for each of the courses. Important note: *I'm not talking about course codes.* These scheduling codes determine the order in which courses are scheduled. We don't have to assign scheduling codes to the singletons; there is no choice as to when they will be scheduled. A list of singletons should be prepared (with their assigned periods) and those periods should be entered *in red* before the process gets under way. If a conflict is discovered between two electives at this stage, it needs to be resolved before the scheduling process begins.

Start with the doubletons; those are the first courses for which there is a choice of sections. If there are five doubletons, then scheduling codes 1, 2, 3, 4, and 5 should be assigned to those courses. Core courses (as opposed to electives) should go first.

Move on to the tripletons. Suppose there are six; then they would be assigned the next six codes: 6, 7, 8, 9, 10, 11. Now move on to those courses that have four, five, and more sections. A sample list of codes appears in Resource C at the end of the book. The codes can be written anywhere on the card.

Step 4: You need a column for keeping track of the "periods available."

Step 5: For each student (scheduling card), circle the subjects that are being taken and enter the scheduling codes in the space provided. This task should be done in advance by several clerically adept people. This same crew could also enter the singletons on the appropriate periods in red. Worth repeating: In preparation for this step, a list of all courses needs to be created with their scheduling codes next to them.

Step 6: You're ready to go. Throw all the cards in a box; don't worry about keeping them in order. They are about to go on an assembly line. Sort the cards by scheduling codes. Pigeonhole mailboxes are helpful for this step. If you don't have them, set up a separate sorting table with large signs for each of the numbers: 1, 2, and so on. By the time you're done sorting all the cards, all the 1's should be in a pile (or box), all the 2's should be in the next pile (or box), and so forth.

Step 7: Suppose that code 1 is the doubleton "Math 10 Honors." One member of the committee is assigned to load that course. It meets periods 3 and 8. The cards are divided up between periods 3 and 8. Keep in mind that the singletons have already been scheduled, so there may be no choice for some cards. It's also possible that for some students *both* periods 3 and 8 are already used; in that case, the card goes into a separate pile/box for conflicts. By the end, the cards in code 1 should be equally divided between periods 3 and 8. The tally goes up on a board looking like this:

1	Math 10 Honors	01	3rd	22
		02	8th	21

Step 9: The committee person must also remember to cross out the 1 in the Scheduling Code column and either the "3" or the "8" in the Available column. Imagine what will happen if she fails to do one or both of these steps. If the code is not crossed out, when the cards are sorted again, this one will end up back in box 1—even though that subject has already been scheduled. If the period is not crossed off, it may be used again later in the process because it appears to be available.

Step 10: Once all the cards have been scheduled for the first subject (scheduling code 1), they can be moved to the next subject. This is done by resorting the cards according to the *next lowest number* in the Codes column. To save time, some schedulers move the cards along to the next code number as soon as they have been processed at the previous station. I prefer to wait until *all* the cards are done. If there is a gross imbalance between the sections at the end, it may be necessary to change some of the period assignments to balance class sizes. Once you've moved the cards along, it's tough, if not impossible, to retrieve them.

Step 11: Another member of the committee begins work on scheduling code 2 . . . Spanish 2 Honors, periods 1 and 5. The process is repeated until every course has been scheduled. Once again, view hand scheduling as an assembly line.

Step 12: It's relatively easy at first with just two sections and most periods available (except for the preassigned singletons). Soon, however, there will be three, four, and more sections. The choice grows greater, but the number of periods available gets smaller. Two, three, or more people may be assigned to work on scheduling those multisection courses. A captain should be appointed to coordinate.

Step 13: At the end of the line, there will be multiple sections to use . . . but correspondingly fewer periods open. You may have a section on every period for a major course, but by this point most students have only one open period on their schedules. What happens, then, if you sort the cards by period availability (a common technique) and discover that only nine can go into the second period section . . . but you have fifty cards that require a seventh period class? You have two options: First, you can determine if any students who need that seventh period class can possibly make a change with one of the subjects already scheduled. Perhaps they were arbitrarily put in a seventh period section, even though another period would have fit just as well. There should be a separate person who is appointed as troubleshooter to deal with this kind of problem. The second option is to make a change in the master schedule at this late date, abolishing that poorly subscribed second period class, reassigning those nine students, and creating a new seventh period class—master schedule permitting. This process is similar to what we did in Step 7 with computer simulation: "Move students . . . move sections."

In theory, you have placed the correct number of sections on each period, but remember what I've said about scheduling not being an exact science. When we talked about the curve of the school, we *approximated* the number of sections needed each period. Because of variable class size (Physical Education, Fine Arts classes, Special Education, and the like), it's rare that the schedule will be perfect at the end, so some adjustment will probably be needed. Expect to make some shifts, even this late in the game.

√ Helpful Hint 47

In addition to the committee members working on the assembly line, there need to be *four* others to assist. These should be the more experienced members. I'm talking about the *trouble-shooter*, who handles problems like the one just described; the person on *conflict patrol*, who deals with scheduling cards that can't be completed because of an unresolved conflict; and the *polisher*, who collects the finished cards and gives them a careful check before they are marked "completed." Someone should also *work the boards* where all the courses and sections are listed. When the tallies come in after a course has been loaded, that person records the number. On the boards, there should be a column for adjustments. For example, a student might be shifted from one section to another. Use a minus sign (−) and a slash (/) next to the tally to keep accurate track of class size. The conflict patrol may have to backtrack and undo some of the scheduling that has already been done. No problem. Even so, there still may be some irresolvable conflicts. *That* can be a problem. Choices may have to be made, even at this late date.

Step 14: When the final code on a card has been crossed out, meaning that the card has been completed and the student is fully scheduled, it should be placed in the "finished" pile/box. At that station, the just-mentioned polisher should be checking that (a) all the subjects have been assigned, (b) there are no conflicts, and (c) there are no gaps.

√ Helpful Hint 48

Add a second (and third) set of periods, in this case 1–8, right next to the first column. The second set is for the polisher, who crosses these numbers off to make sure that the student has a complete schedule. The third is for the triple and final check.

1	1	1
2	2	2
3	3	3
4	4	4
5	5	5
6	6	6
7	7	7
8	8	8

Step 15: When the last card has reached the finished pile/box and been checked by the polisher, it's time for that *triple* check. Everyone on the committee should sit with a pile of cards and go through them one more time, checking for errors: conflicts, omissions, gaps, and so on. One technique is to count periods, starting with the first—making sure that there is one subject assigned from first to last period.

The process is now complete. The cards can be sorted alphabetically, by homeroom, by counselor, or any other way that works for your school.

Method 3—By Arena: The least common method for loading students is by arena. Some schools have returned to this old-fashioned, college-style scheduling.

Arena scheduling is a student-self scheduling system in which students load themselves into the schedule—rather than having the computer do it for them. The ten scheduling steps presented in this book are still followed. However, the difference comes at Step 8 where there is a detour. Everything is the same up to this point. Now the loading of students into sections by the computer is bypassed. The students receive a copy of the master and develop several workable schedules for themselves. The significant difference is that they are no longer at the mercy of the computer; nor are they passive in the process. They are *actively* involved in the decision-making. Arena scheduling requires a tremendous amount of planning and groundwork, but administrators who have adopted it claim that the benefits accrued are worth the effort.

Modified Arena: Some schools have adopted certain aspects of arena scheduling. One is arena-by-exception, in which students get a computer-generated schedule and are permitted to make one or two requests for changes to tailor it to their liking. The setup is far simpler. It can be done one of two ways: first, by mail, filling out a form and returning it to the counselor who reviews the request; second, in person, by appointment time, in the Guidance suite or library. You must make sure that all of the necessary materials, as well as access to computers, are available for the counselors as they meet with students. Arena-by-exception is a compromise. It doesn't entail all the work of the full-blown Arena, but it reaps some of the dividends.

A second version involves having the computer lock in the core courses (English, Math, etc.). Since it's the singleton electives that tend to cause conflicts, students then receive appointment times, much like the arena-by-exception, to meet with counselors and slot in electives around the core courses, using a list of electives listed by period. We tend to have arena scheduling *de facto*. When students receive notification that there are conflicts, they end up changing the electives anyway. Why not make it *de jure* and schedule the electives arena-style from the start? Just be aware that there is one flaw: Electives were formed based on tallies. Changes at this point are on a space-available basis only.

Summary

There is just so much tinkering you can do. Once you are satisfied that the master schedule is the very best that it can be, it's time to lock it and load the students into the sections. There are three very different ways to do this: (1) by hand, (2) by computer, and (3) by arena. There are distinct advantages and disadvantages in all three methods. Your situation and set of circumstances will determine which is right for you. If you are not totally satisfied with the method you are using, your scheduling committee might want to do a feasibility study to determine if one of the other two methods is better.

Although arena scheduling is not in widespread use, it offers a number of benefits. Two modified versions of arena scheduling were suggested that allow some of those benefits to still be accrued without adopting the concept completely.

As different as the three methods are, they share a common denominator: Lock in singletons . . . then go to doubletons . . . tripletons . . . and ultimately the multisection courses. It is sheer logic, no matter whether you schedule by hand, arena, or computer. As the number of sections increases . . . the number of available periods decreases, because they have been locked up already by courses that offer little or no choice.

TASKS FOR STEP 8

- Lock the master schedule and go to "maintenance."
- Determine which is the best method for loading students into sections.
- Whichever method you elect, prepare the scheduling materials to get the job done.
- Actually load the students into the schedule—by computer, by hand, or by arena.
- Take some time to carefully check the schedules for accuracy before distributing them.
- Prepare a set of those schedules to be sent home for review by students and parents.
- Provide a mechanism for students to indicate any *legitimate* errors in the schedules.
- Consider a feasibility study on whether arena scheduling, or any of its components, would serve your school well.

Step 9

Adjust It

Mop-Up: End-of-Year Changes

You're almost finished—but not quite. The master schedule has been built . . . tested . . . tinkered with . . . and loaded. Schedules for the next school year have been distributed. What else is there to do? Some polishing needs to be done before the current school year ends and the new one gets under way. Actually, there are *two* times to make *adjustments*. The first one comes just prior to school letting out for the summer.

1. Requests for Changes

When you mailed home schedules earlier in the month, you gave students a chance to review them and request legitimate changes. They may have picked up on *legitimate* errors you missed in terms of courses, course levels, "tracks" (honors, AP, remedial, etc.), electives, and the like. Note that I said legitimate. On the course change form, we were very clear that requests for teacher changes . . . lunch period changes . . . and course changes are verboten at this point.

2. Reversals

This could be major. Students were programmed based on their progress in current courses, whether they were passing or failing at midyear. We deliberately delayed the start of Step 4 (the course selection process) until the start of the second semester to give students, parents, and counselors midyear grades before choosing courses for the following year. But that was more than four months ago; a great deal could have happened since. A student who was passing a course . . . may have taken a nosedive and is now failing it; conversely, a student who appeared to be hopelessly failing a course may have made a miraculous recovery to end up passing. The counselor had programmed based on the status at midyear. Now, an adjustment has to be made. For example, if a student had been passing Spanish 2 at midyear but ended up failing it . . . obviously the Spanish 3 must be dropped and he must be reprogrammed to repeat Spanish 2. But is there space in Spanish 2? What happens if there are many such last-minute reversals? How will they affect both the Spanish 2 and Spanish 3 sections?

Remember that crystal ball we used for determining the number of sections per course? Get it out again. Counselors frequently have to make close calls as to how to program marginal students. Their passing or failing a course at the last minute can have an impact on their courses and schedules for the following year.

3. Conflicts

Believe it or not, there still *may* be some conflicts on the schedules. How can this happen, given all the supposed fail-safe checks? Some do manage to escape the scheduler, however, and some are created by those last-minute section shifts during simulation. As you get more experienced, there should be fewer to resolve this late in the game. In any event, don't be surprised if some pop up.

4. Clerical Errors

You also may be surprised to find that there are still clerical errors that need to be corrected: invalid course codes, canceled courses still appearing on the schedules, incorrect dummy codes (lunch, study halls, early dismissal, etc.). These are relatively easy to deal with; just make sure to address them.

5. New Admits

Before school lets out, you may already be aware of new admits for the coming year. Some districts schedule students one at a time as they register in the spring; others hold off until the opening of school. A major variable is mobility. Across the fifty states, there is quite a range. In some areas, school closes and opens with virtu- ally the identical school population; there is little moving in and moving out of the dis- trict. In other regions of the country, there is tremendous mobility, with a large number of new admits arriving for the new year. The experienced scheduler will get a sense of his school's pattern. I worked in an urban school that learned to plan for a large last-minute influx of ninth graders each fall. Whatever you decide, clear-cut poli- cies and procedures need to be developed for registering and scheduling new admits.

6. Discharges ("Lefts" and "Exits")

Similarly, you'll learn about students who are leaving the district. Their sched- ules should be pulled quickly to open up spaces in sections that might have been closed. As with new admits, the number of discharges from year to year may run the gamut. It is not an issue for some districts, while it is a major one for others. And as with new admits, with experience you will be able to make some projections as to changes in the size of your student population.

Implications

Listed above are six very different types of adjustments you may have to make before the close of the school year. Notice that they share a common denominator that you must watch closely: *What effect will they have on section size?* You worked long and hard to make sure that (1) you had the correct number of sections for each course, and (2) the class sizes across multisection courses were balanced. Now, for a variety of reasons, there have been last-minute changes:

First, let's review the genesis of those changes:

- Students placed in incorrect levels or tracks of courses
- Students in wrong electives
- Students with irresolvable conflicts who need another subject
- Students with clerical errors who are missing a subject
- Students who were passing courses . . . but are now failing them
- Students who were failing courses . . . but are now passing them
- Students who are new to the district . . . and need a brand new schedule
- Students who are leaving the district . . . and are opening up spaces

Your carefully constructed master may take a bit of a beating at this point. When the dust settles, you may find that your section sizes are highly imbalanced. This is to be expected. What do you do? Carefully review your most up-to-date sections list showing class sizes. See if there are any egregious cases: Can you absorb students into the existing sections? Can you retain sections that have *lost* students? At this point, you may have to make some adjustments, abolishing some sections while creating others. Suppose that fifteen students unexpectedly failed Math 2 at the last minute—and you just don't have fifteen spaces in Math 2 next year for them to repeat the course. You may be able to collapse the sections of Math 3 for next year and convert a Math 3 to a Math 2. Consult the Math schedule and make any changes in concert with the department head.

For some schools, these are ongoing problems, and they plan for these changes when the master schedule is built. For example, suppose Earth Science is offered in the ninth grade, and suppose that it historically has a high failure rate. The experienced scheduler would be aware of this fact and return to Step 4 when she must decide on the number of sections for Earth Science . . . and Biology, the tenth grade course. Based on the history, she decides on one fewer section of Biology and one more section of Earth Science than the numbers indicate. Based on her experience, she builds in the growing room for those failures.

Another district has a different problem with Earth Science in the ninth grade. Year after year, by October, every one of the Earth Science sections was at capacity due to the last-minute enrollment of new admits when school opened. After a few years, the scheduler was prepared and provided growing room for the newly arriving ninth graders, not only in Earth Science, but in other ninth grade classes, too.

Still a third example comes from Special Education. Placing classified students was complicated by two factors: (1) Class sizes are capped much lower, ergo, more sensitive to last-minute changes, and (2) placements are made *after* the master schedule is built. By the time elective requests are received, many popular classes are filled. The scheduler must learn from experience to hold places and build in growing room.

> **√ Helpful Hint 49**
>
> During Step 9 (and Step 10, to follow), log any changes you make to the master schedule based on enrollment changes. For example: Add a section of Earth Science, convert a Spanish 3 to a Spanish 2, and so on. *Save the record of these modifications for next year.* This information could prove very useful in the future when there are tough calls as to the number of sections to run. See in which direction those courses went *after* the section decisions were made. For example, if you are on the cusp of whether to offer five or six sections of English 10 and your notes indicate that you had to add a section last year, then go with six. Even if it doesn't turn out to be the correct call *this* year, at least it was an informed decision.

Summary

And you thought you were finished after Step 8. Step 9, Adjust It, is a mop-up, clean-up, polishing step at the end of the school year when unanticipated changes have to be made. With experience, however, fewer of those changes should be unanticipated as the scheduler foresees them and builds them into the schedule.

The school year comes to an end. Yes, there is rest for the weary. Take some time off over the summer. But wait: You're not quite through yet. There is one final step before the opening day of school for next year.

TASKS FOR STEP 9

- Review requests for changes submitted by students when they received their schedules.
- Have counselors give schedules a final check for errors, omissions, and the like.
- Call for last-minute grade reversals: fail to pass, pass to fail.
- Set up a formalized procedure for registering new admits and deleting students who are leaving.

Step 10

Refine It

The Final Touch-Up

As mentioned in the previous step, there are *two* opportunities to polish the schedules before the new school year begins. The second comes just before opening day. In most districts, time is allotted prior to the first day of school for counselors to make last-minute *refinements*. Step 10 is similar to Step 9—except that you have additional information by the end of summer. Changes now fall into just two categories:

- *Summer School (if you have one):* Once again, adjustments may have to be made in students' schedules based on their unanticipated going/not going to summer school and their unanticipated passing/failing the courses they did take. Follow the same procedures as in Step 9 and adjust their schedules accordingly based on the new information. Let's hope there will be spaces available in the sections you need. Otherwise, you may have to revisit the master schedule yet again to make changes.
- *New Admits/Discharges:* Depending on the mobility factor in your district, you may have new students to register . . . and current students to release. These changes could also significantly impact your existing section sizes.

Now, at last your scheduling for the new school year is done. It is imperative that you receive updated lists of section sizes during this period. A Helpful Hint in an earlier chapter suggested that this report be published on a daily basis as opening day approaches. With all the changes, you may spot some new irregularities in section size:

- Sections far too small
- Sections far too big
- Imbalanced sections in multisection courses

It's back to the drawing board one final time before school opens. You may have to add some sections, abolish others, and balance still others by shifting students. In the worst case scenario, you won't be able to collapse sections in one subject while you need one (or more) in another. Let's say that you desperately need another section of English 10. You have four sections of English 11 with the following registers: seventeen, sixteen, fifteen, and nineteen. (The cap is 25.) You could *easily* drop from four to three sections. Unfortunately, the students' schedules aren't cooperating. In other words, there is no one section that can be eliminated without displacing a large number of students. You may *have* to keep all four. After all, this is *not* the students' fault—and it is unreasonable to have them disrupt their schedules at this late date. In a case like this one, just hope that some contingency money has been budgeted and you have an understanding superintendent. Be prepared to beg . . . and even grovel.

Is it ever reasonable to upset a student's schedule? Suppose that after the school year has begun it is agreed that a student doesn't belong in an honors class after all; it had been a borderline placement to begin with. It is decided to let him drop down to a regular class, but the only open section entails a major overhaul of his schedule. The only other alternative is to change a *different* student's schedule just to accommodate this one. That's not fair, just to satisfy his change of heart.

Countdown to Opening Day

As opening day approaches, continue to watch section sizes on a regular basis, the way a stockbroker follows the Dow Jones. Abolish sections . . . create sections . . . balance sections . . . shift students—as needed. Ideally, these moves will be kept to the bare minimum. At the last possible moment, print a complete run of revised schedules to be mailed home just before opening day or distributed in school on the first day.

√ Helpful Hint 50

Up to now, we've been concerned primarily with student schedules, and to some degree, teacher schedules. There is a host of *other* valuable reports that most scheduling software packages generate at this time, including:

- Room utilization charts
- Oversubscribed classes
- Undersubscribed classes (you set the threshold)
- Room conflict report
- Teacher conflict report

Become familiar with all of the tools at your fingertips. What's available varies from system to system, but some tools are common to all. Review them all. They can help you anticipate any last-minute problems and do any fine-tuning still necessary.

Your job is now officially done. Well, for the moment, anyway. On opening day, run it . . . watch it . . . and (sigh), get ready to start all over again. It's already time to begin work on Step 1—building the master schedule for the *following* school year.

Summary

Step 10 is similar to Step 9, except that it comes after summer school and just before the opening of school, and the bulk of new admits has arrived. It's one last opportunity to give the master a final, last-minute once-over, refine the schedules, abolish and create classes, and balance sections.

TASKS FOR STEP 10

This is your last chance to do the following:

- Adjust schedules based on summer school results.
- Process last-minute new admits and discharges.
- Fine-tune sections in the master schedule as needed.
- Balance section registers.
- Print and distribute the updated student and teacher schedules, rosters, room utilization charts, and the like.
- Sit back . . . bask in the glory of your handiwork . . . and get ready to start all over again.

Final Word

As I said at the outset, building the master schedule is a ten-step, twelve-month process. Many would-be administrators shy away from this job because it is so overwhelming. The goal of this book is to make the process less threatening and laborious and more manageable and understandable. As I also mentioned at the beginning, during the introductions at my workshops I always ask the participants *why* they've come. Over the past thirty years, I've gotten some pretty hilarious answers, but the denominator common to all of them is that nobody else wanted the job: They're either low on the totem pole or have to pay their dues—and now they are stuck with it.

I hope that after using this text, you won't feel stuck, but will see that the job is certainly doable. In addition, it can be fun and it can be rewarding. Perhaps the best advice I can give at this point is to repeat those three skills requisite for administrators: conceptual . . . technical . . . interpersonal. Remember that a three-legged stool needs three legs to stand. Two are not enough; it will topple. So it is with these three skills. All three are requisites for scheduling success.

Building the master schedule is both a science *and* an art. With experience, you will pick up more tricks of the trade; I know I did, even while preparing this book. I tried to pass along those hints, techniques, and tips. Still others you will acquire by doing, once you assume the job. You never stop learning in the scheduling business.

I will conclude the way I started: A master schedule reveals a great deal about its school. Do everything you can to make sure that yours is the very best it can possibly be.

Resource A

10-Step Review

We've now completed the ten steps in building the master schedule. We have gone through the scheduling cycle, from September to the following September—just in time to start all over again. A tremendous amount of material has been covered. Let's review by step . . . by month . . . by document. Keep in mind that school systems operating on an August–May cycle need to move things up by a month. Internal factors may also temper your timeline. No problem. Adjust the deadlines; the content remains the same.

BY STEP

Step 1. Plan It

The curriculum review process kicks off the ten-step process in *October* and is completed by *Thanksgiving*. A curriculum review council or scheduling committee is convened to review the present course of study and make recommendations for adding, dropping, and modifying courses.

Step 2. Package It

Once the course of study has been agreed upon, *December* is devoted to detail work. This step is broken down into four parts: course codes, course titles, course descriptions, and course catalogues. These materials must be prepared "backstage" before the curtain goes up on the scheduling process.

Step 3. Market It

Right after *New Year's Day*, it is time to disseminate information to students and parents. A "Curriculum Fair" is recommended, done jointly with one or more of the other methods. It is important to "hype" the process (the way *TV Guide* promotes the new fall season) so that students and parents give it the attention it deserves.

Step 4. Count 'Em Up

Up to this point, information has gone one way: from the school to students and parents. Now information flows the other way, during *February and the first half of March.* The value of a "course selection contract" in which students see their choices as *commitments* is underscored. On or around *St. Patrick's Day* the scheduler receives two documents, one of which is the master tally, used to determine the number of sections for each course. A simple equation—tallies become sections . . . and sections become staff—governs the decisions. Once the number of sections has been decided, the department heads develop a course load for each teacher.

Step 5. Spot Trouble

By *early April* it's time to start constructing the master. But there is a critical preliminary step that must come first. The conflict matrix is the second document delivered with the tally. It is used to ascertain which courses students are commonly taking in tandem so that these courses can be placed on different periods. Various formats for the conflict matrix were shown to make the arduous task less cumbersome.

Step 6. Build It

Placement of singletons based on information yielded by the conflict matrix provides the skeleton of the master schedule. By *mid-April* it is time to flesh out the schedule with all the other sections. Factors to consider when building the schedule were enumerated; careful thought has to be given to the placement of every single section. The domino effect resulting when even one section is moved was demonstrated. Four methods for approaching this task were detailed; exercises were provided to give schedulers the skills needed to get the job done.

Step 7. Test It

Once the master schedule is complete, it's time to test it during *May.* Thanks to computer simulation, we get a "report card" showing the percentage of students successfully scheduled. Improvements can be made by moving students . . . moving sections . . . and changing priority numbers (the order in which courses are scheduled). Try, try, try again. There is no limit to the number of runs, because "100 percent" is the target.

Step 8. Load It

By the *end of May* it's time to stop making changes and *lock* the master schedule. Everyone connected with scheduling must know when this switch is thrown. Changes can still be made, but the procedure is different under "maintenance." Now it's time to load the students into sections: by hand, by computer, or by arena. Each method has its advantages and disadvantages. All three share a common approach: Start with the hardest-to-schedule (singleton) classes first . . . and work up to the easiest-to-schedule classes (those with multiple sections), keeping in mind that there is less choice toward the end of the process. After a final check for correctness, schedules are mailed home to students and parents before the end of the school year.

Step 9. Adjust It

There are still some adjustments that have to be made at the *close of the school year*. In addition to responding to legitimate student concerns after schedules were sent home, counselors must clean up remaining conflicts, clerical errors, and pass–fail reversals as well as deal with new admits and with discharges.

Step 10. Refine It

The second "mop up" or "polishing" takes place during the *summer*, just before school reopens, and takes into account two more sources of changes: summer school and additional new admits/discharges. The scheduler needs to watch the sections list on a daily basis and be prepared to abolish, create, and balance sections.

No sooner has the tenth step been completed, when it is time to run the schedule . . . watch the schedule . . . (sigh) . . . and get ready to start all over again.

Now let's turn things around and work our way through the calendar, month by month. It's the same ten steps, only this time organized by year.

Resource B

10-Step Review by Month of the School Year

Remember: As explained in the Introduction, this timeline will have to be adjusted slightly for school systems on an August-to-June calendar. The tasks, however, remain exactly the same.

September

School opens, schedules are given out, and classes begin. Sit back, at least for the moment, and watch your handiwork from the previous year. Notify faculty that ideas for new courses must be submitted to department heads now.

October—Mid-November

Kick off the scheduling cycle for the *next* school year by convening the curriculum advisory council and/or scheduling committee to review the course of study *(Step 1)*.

December

The curriculum review is behind you . . . the scheduling process for students is just ahead. This month is reserved for meticulously preparing all the scheduling materials that will be used *(Step 2)*: course codes, titles, descriptions, and a knockout course catalogue.

January

It's time to go public with considerable fanfare to stir interest in scheduling.
Engage students and parents *(Step 3)* through a variety of methods to hype the process.
Unveil the new course of study at a curriculum fair or in some other exciting way.

February—Early March

On your mark, get set, go! As soon as first-semester grades have been posted . . . start taking course requests for next year. Add 'em up . . . to produce the master tally.

Late March

Decide on the number of sections to be offered for each and every course (*Step 4*). Department heads use these numbers to carve out a course load for each teacher.

Early April

Start with the conflict matrix (*Step 5*) to "spot trouble."
Separate those singleton courses that clusters of students are taking in tandem.
The placement of these singletons becomes the skeleton of the master schedule.

Mid-April

Flesh out the skeleton—and place all of the other sections in the master schedule. Considerable thought goes into the placement of each and every section (*Step 6*).

May

Computer simulation (*Step 7*) provides feedback about the schedule.
Clear up problems now, before school opens, so it can be "business as usual" from day one of the school year.

June 1

The final simulation is completed and the master schedule is locked.
Students are loaded into the schedule by hand, by computer, or by arena (*Step 8*).
Schedules are printed and sent home for review by students and parents.

Late June

Before school breaks, legitimate adjustments are made (*Step 9*), including . . . unresolved conflicts, clerical errors, pass–fail reversals, new admits, and discharges.

August

With school about to open, counselors are on hand for last-minute changes (*Step 10*): summer school and/or additional new admits and discharges.
The scheduler monitors section sizes to abolish, create, and balance sections as needed. At the very last moment, revised schedules are printed and readied for distribution.

September

Students pick up their schedules on opening day . . . and it's time to start all over again!

Resource C

10-Step Review by Document

The third and final review reinforces the ten steps once more, this time by offering a sample document representing each of the steps. For several, there is more than one that could have been included; I have chosen the one that I deem to be most representative of that step.

Step 1. Plan It   Curriculum Council's recommendations

Step 2. Package It   Course Selection *Contract*

Step 3. Market It   Invitation to the Annual Curriculum Fair

Step 4. Count 'Em Up   Master Tally

Step 5. Spot Trouble   Honors and Advanced Placement Courses—Conflict Matrix

Step 6. Build It   Draft of Foreign Language Department Schedule

Step 7. Test It   Simulation Data

Step 8. Load It   Coding Sheet for Hand Loading

Step 9. Adjust It   Pass–Fail Reversals Report

Step 10. Refine It   Summer School Report

Step 1. Plan It: Curriculum Development

Excerpts From Summary Of Curriculum Council's Recommendations

Introduction. Building the master schedule is a ten-step, twelve-month process that runs from October to October. The first step is what we call the "menu-planning" phase: curriculum review. For six weeks during the fall, the Principal's Cabinet changes hats and becomes the "Curriculum Council," undertaking a complete review of our school's course of study, asking three questions: *What should be added? What should be deleted? What should be modified?* What follows is a summary of the recommendations that were agreed upon—and that now will be passed on to the Superintendent and ultimately the Board of Education for review and, hopefully, approval. I would like to take this opportunity to thank all of the members of the Council who undertook this responsibility. . . .

The **ENGLISH** Department would like to add a Research course similar to the one offered by the Science and Social Studies Departments. It will be aimed at eleventh and twelfth grade Honors and Advanced Placement students to provide a "launching pad" for those interested in writing, literary analysis, and research. At the same time, the department is recommending removing the "Sports in Literature" elective that has failed to make the cut for the past three years. . . . The **SOCIAL STUDIES** Department would like to add an elective in "Cultural Anthropology." The Advanced Placement Program does not offer such a course, we will therefore develop the curriculum in conjunction with one of the local colleges. To make room for this new course, the "Human Geography" elective, which has been poorly subscribed for the past two years, will be deleted from the course of study. . . . The **MATH** Department would like to replace the "Computer Programming" course with a "Computer Applications" elective that will be useful to all students. Originally, the **BUSINESS** Department wanted this course to be under its aegis; however, since it is replacing the Programming course, it was agreed that it should fall under the Math Department. In addition, the highly successful double-period program (currently offered to marginal students in Math 9 and Math 10) will be extended to the eleventh grade. Finally, the Math Department is exploring the feasibility of converting the present half-year Statistics elective to either a full-year Advanced Placement Statistics course or a full-year course affiliated with one of the local colleges. . . . The **FOREIGN LANGUAGE** Department will be renamed the **"WORLD LANGUAGES"** Department. In addition, it is proposing a new one-year **"Introduction** to Spanish" course for students who heretofore have shied away from language study. This will *not* be a sequence course; at present it is for just one year. We will revisit the course at this time next year to consider extending it. It will be open to Special Education students as well. . . .

Step 2. Package It: Preparing Scheduling Materials

Course Selection Contract

Dear Student,

You are about to select your courses for next year. We can't stress strongly enough how important this process is. No longer is the form we use called the "Course Selection Worksheet"; it is now called the *"Course Selection **Contract**.*" Based on your requests, classes are formed and teachers are assigned. If twenty-five students sign up for an elective, we make one class; if seventy-six students sign up for an elective, we make three classes.

Considering the number of courses we offer, imagine what would happen if each and every student had a change of mind later on. We want you to understand the problems that could cause and to realize that we're not unreasonable when we say "no!" to a course change later in the process. Have you ever gone to a banquet where the waiter asked what you would like to eat: chicken? fish? roast beef? Based on everyone's requests, the chef gets to work preparing the meals. Now imagine what would happen if, after ordering fish, you sat down for dinner and told the waiter you really wanted roast beef. *There would be chaos in the kitchen!*

So it is with course requests. Based on what you tell us you want, we form classes and assign teachers. Don't think of us as mean when we deny requests for changes that would cause overcrowding in some classes and imbalances in others. To put it another way, we can't afford to run out of roast beef and have all that leftover fish!

Thank you for your understanding.

I have read and understand this "contract."

_____

(student signature)

Step 3. Market It: Disseminating Information

Invitation to Curriculum Fair

USA High School
cordially invites all students and parents to its—

Annual Curriculum Fair
Monday, January 11, at 7:30 PM

as we launch the scheduling process for the next school year!

*Introduction to the Course Selection Process (Auditorium)

*What's New for Next Year? (Auditorium)

*Changes in the Graduation Requirements (Auditorium)

*Grade-Level Meetings With Counselors:

Next year's ninth graders—remain in the Auditorium

Next year's tenth graders—conference center

Next year's eleventh graders—library

Next year's twelfth graders—band room

*Curriculum Fair (cafeteria)

Visit tables and exhibits for all our subject departments.

*Our new course catalogue will be given out this evening.

*Refreshments will be served, courtesy of the Key Club

Circle the date: Be sure to be with us on January 11th.

Step 4. Count 'Em Up: Determining the Number of Sections

Master Tally

Code	Title	Total	Boys	Girls	09*	10*	11*	12*
111	English 9S	37	19	18	29	8	0	0
112	English 9R	180	89	91	162	17	1	0
113	English 9H	53	25	28	53	0	0	0
121	English 10S	45	22	23	3	40	2	0
122	English 10R	190	90	100	8	178	3	1
123	English 10H	60	31	29	0	60	0	0
131	English 11S	41	20	21	0	5	29	7
132	English 11R	184	92	92	0	10	174	0
133	English 11H	68	33	35	0	0	68	0
141	English 12S	36	16	20	0	0	4	32
142	English 12R	169	85	84	0	0	7	162
143	English 12H	27	13	14	0	0	0	27
144	English 12AP	16	8	8	0	0	0	16
151	Journalism	24	10	14	0	6	7	11
152	Creative Writing	47	22	25	0	15	14	18
153	Shakespeare	9	4	5	0	0	3	6
154	Public Speaking	33	17	16	0	7	9	17
155	World Drama	22	11	11	0	0	7	15
161	Writing Lab	55	27	28	31	20	4	0
162	Reading Lab	63	32	31	33	27	3	0
163	SAT Prep	84	42	42	0	6	68	10

Note: *Grades 9–12 reflect school's promotion policy regarding number of credits earned to be officially promoted to next grade.

Conflict Matrix

This is a custom matrix. The computer was programmed to include only Advanced Placement courses for tenth, eleventh, and twelfth grades.

	World History	Biology	American History	Chemistry	English	Economics	Government	Calculus	Statistics	Physics	Spanish	French
World History	—	2	0	0	0	0	0	3	3	0	0	0
Biology	2	—	7	3	0	0	0	0	4	0	0	0
American History	0	7	—	4	0	0	0	0	1	0	0	0
Chemistry	0	3	4	—	3	0	0	2	7	2	1	0
English	0	0	0	3	—	10	9	7	5	3	2	3
Economics	0	0	0	0	10	—	17	12	8	3	4	1
Government	0	0	0	0	9	17	—	9	5	1	5	0
Calculus	3	0	0	2	7	12	9	—	3	3	4	1
Statistics	3	4	1	7	5	8	5	3	—	2	0	1
Physics	0	0	0	2	3	3	1	3	2	—	2	0
Spanish	0	0	0	1	2	4	5	4	0	2	—	0
French	0	0	0	0	3	1	0	1	1	0	0	—

Step 6. Build It: Placing Sections in the Schedule

Draft of Foreign Language Department Master Schedule

	1st	2nd	3rd	4th	5th	6th	7th	8th
Ms. A. Ames (103)	Spanish 2	Spanish 3		Spanish 2	Spanish 3H		Spanish 2	
Mr. B. Bell (101)		Spanish 1	Spanish 2	Spanish 1		Spanish 2		Spanish 3
Dr. C. Craig (104)	French 2		French AP		French 3	French 4		French 1
Mr. D. Davis (102)	Spanish 1 (101)	Spanish 2H (102)	Spanish 1 (102)			MIDDLE SCHOOL	MIDDLE SCHOOL	MIDDLE SCHOOL
Ms. E. Eng (102)	Spanish 3			Spanish 3	Latin 2		Latin 3	Latin 1
Ms. F. Fish	Asst. Dean	Asst. Dean				Spanish 4 (103)	Spanish AP (104)	Spanish 4 (103)

Except for Assistant Dean, the duties, lunch, preparation periods, and so on can be added later.

Step 7. Test It: Computer Simulation

Simulation Data (Excerpts for HEALTH EDUCATION)

Section	Period	Semester	Teacher	Load	Maximum	Open
01	01	Fall	R. Simmons	28	30	2
02	02	Spring	R. Simmons	30	30	0
03	03	Fall	R. Simmons	26	30	4
04	03	Spring	R. Simmons	22	30	8
05	04	Spring	R. Simmons	14	30	16
06	05	Fall	R. Simmons	30	30	0
07	06	Fall	R. Simmons	31	30	-1*
08	07	Spring	R. Simmons	30	30	0
09	08	Fall	R. Simmons	12	30	18
10	08	Spring	R. Simmons	18	30	12

229 out of 272 requests scheduled

60 seats still open

*Indicates an "override" by administrator to go above class size maximum

Note: The simulation data indicate that Health Education needs a great deal of work.

- A total of forty-three students are still not scheduled for this course.
- There is plenty of room in six of the sections, but obviously these won't work for those students; otherwise they would have been placed in them.
- It would be interesting to lift the caps on the closed sections in order to see how many more students could be accommodated.
- Perhaps one or more of the sections could be moved to other periods where they would load better.

Step 8. Load It: Computer, Hand, and Arena Loading Systems

Coding Sheet for Hand Loading

(Code indicates the order in which the course is scheduled. Singletons were scheduled in advance and do not appear here. Lowest codes go to doubletons, tripletons, etc.)

Course	Code	Number	Periods
English 9G	1	2	3 6
Italian 1	2	2	5 8
Technology	3	2	4 7
Earth Science G	4	3	4 6 9
Music Appreciation	5	4	2 3 7 8
Math 9G	6	5	1 4 5 6 8
Studio Art	7	6	4 5 6 7 8 9
Math 9R	8	7	1 3 4 6 7 8 9
Earth Science R	9	8	2 3 4 5 6 7 8 9
Spanish 1	10	9	2 3 4 5 6 7 8 9 10
English 9	11	10	1 2 3 4 5 6 7 8 9 10
Physical Education	12	11	1 2 3 4 5 6 7 8 8 9 10
Social Studies	13	12	1 2 2 3 3 4 5 6 7 8 9 10

Notes:

- This school has a ten-period day.
- Students are on one of three sessions: 1–8, 2–9, or 3–10.
- As the code gets higher (from 1 to 13), the number of sections *increases.*
- However, as has been stated, the number of open periods on a student's schedule *decreases.*
- For Physical Education and Social Studies, there are so many sections that there are two on some periods.

Step 9. Adjust It: End-of-the-Year Changes

Summary of Year-End Reversals by Department: Science

Fail to Pass	Earth Science	Biology	Chemistry	Physics
A. Einstein	0	2	0	0
B. Pasteur	1	1	0	0
C. Curie	0	2	3	0
D. Pascal	0	0	2	0
E. Euclid	0	0	0	2
Totals:	**1**	**5**	**5**	**2**

Pass to Fail	Earth Science	Biology	Chemistry	Physics
A. Einstein	7	3	0	0
B. Pasteur	4	3	0	0
C. Curie	0	4	5	0
D. Pascal	0	0	7	0
E. Euclid	0	0	0	5
Totals:	**11**	**10**	**12**	**5**

Notes: The students who were failing but are now passing must be advanced to the next subject. For example, if the counselor had originally scheduled an Earth Science student to repeat Earth Science, she must now take him out of Earth Science and move him on to Biology.

On the other hand, students who were passing but are now failing must be taken out of the new course and repeat the course they failed (unless, of course, there is a provision for summer school).

Most important: Look at the totals. The numbers of sections for these four courses were based on the original tallies. Can the current sections absorb these new students—or—will there have to be some adjustment to the master schedule?

Step 10. Refine It:
Last-Minute Polishing Before School Reopens

Summary School Report

To: Counselors

From: Scheduling Office

The following students attended summer school; listed below is the pass–fail report. Adjust their schedules for the new school year accordingly, based on these results.

Note: As with the pass–fail reversal report at the end of the school year, the summer school report at the end of the summer is used to adjust student schedules and determine whether they can be accommodated in the present schedule. Once again, it may be necessary to make some modifications in the master schedule.

Andrews, Jack	English 9 (P)	Earth Science (F)
Bridges, Mindy	Social Studies 9 (P)	Earth Science (P)
Chu, Carl	Math 9 (F)	Spanish 1 (P)
Dwyer, Dina	Math 9 (P)	Earth Science (P)
Eagle, Howard	English 9 (F)	Math 9 (F)
Fernandez, Jose	Math 9 (F)	Earth Science 9 (F)
Garber, Jane	English 9 (F)	Earth Science (P)
Howe, Fred	Earth Science (P)	
Ivers, Linda	Math 9 (P)	Earth Science (P)
Jones, Paul	Social Studies 9 (P)	
King, Sarah	Math 9 (F)	Spanish 1 (P)
Lewis, Tad	Spanish 1 (P)	
Mills, Yolanda	English 9 (P)	Social Studies 9 (P)
Nathan, Edward	English 9 (F)	Math 9 (P)
Owens, Penny	Earth Science (P)	
Poe, Calvin	Math 9 (P)	Earth Science (P)

Printed in the United States
By Bookmasters